My Above Average Colon

January Ornellas

Cover: Design by Dwayne Booth

Book layout by HumorOutcasts Press.

Published 2023 by HumorOutcasts Press

Printed in the United States of America

ISBN: 979-8-9894863-1-1

For my dad, who is the reason I became a writer

Contents

Chapter 1 - Dysfunctional Family Fun

A family is essential to provide love and support. And good material.

My Nest Runneth Over

My pregnant daughter, Quincey, son-in-law, Colby, and their two dogs moved in with us recently.

The first week was wonderful; no arguments, no misunderstandings, not so much as a snarky comment was uttered.

Pure bliss.

Of course, my husband, Steve, and I were on vacation the first week.

The second week was trickier.

It was all seven of us (four adults, three dogs) living under one quarantined roof.

Like Alcatraz, with puppies.

Some days were better than others.

Sometimes it was all of us laughing, joking, and cooking together.

At other times, I was a raving lunatic because NOBODY KNOWS HOW TO TAKE OUT THE TRASH!

Correction: They knew how to take out the trash, but…

"I normally don't take out the trash until it's full," Colby informed me.

I eyed the mound of garbage bursting from its white plastic exterior.

I guess we had different definitions of full.

Sometimes, we took the dogs for a walk and enjoyed the crisp spring evening together.

Other times, the puppies were busy redecorating my rug.

I tried not to lose my mind as Quincey and Colby launched an investigation into which dog was the actual "Poopetrator."

"Was it you, Buttons?"*

No response.

"Charlie, did you do this?"

Silence.

They waited patiently for an answer, but clearly, these mutts were taking the fifth.

This didn't deter them, and the Q and A continued. (Actually, it was all Q, no A.)

"Which one of you was it?"

Still, no A.

They eyed the pups, voices stern. "Somebody is going in their crate!"

Did it have to be a dog?

Sometimes, we'd celebrate Quincey's pregnancy by placing a piece of fruit on the table to signify the size of the growing baby. Last week, it was a grapefruit.

We all oohed and aahed over the miracle of life!

Other times, that fruit turned into a mixer.

Eying the empty bowl, Quincey yelled, "Who ate my baby?!"

I sipped my greyhound.

I have no idea.

Sometimes, we snuggled on the couch, watching *Tommy Boy*, just for the fun of it.

Other times, we were on the couch, watching *Knives Out*, just for the…

Uh, oh…It appeared some of us were taking notes.

Should I be concerned?

*Names have been changed to protect the canines

Have I Taught You Nothing?

In my fifty-four years, I thought I had garnered a few pearls of wisdom.

Turns out my pearls of wisdom were actually nuggets of nonsense.

Especially when it came to raising children.

Thankfully, my oldest daughter, Quincey, set me straight.

It started the first time I changed my granddaughter, Holland. I had just pulled out the powder when Quincey flew across the room.

"NOOOOOOO!" She grabbed the container from my hands. "You can't use that!"

This was confusing because, well… *it was <u>BABY</u> powder.*

She retrieved a box of cornstarch from her diaper bag. "Cornstarch is better because it doesn't have talc."

"Is talc bad?"

Deep sighs.

How poor Quincey had raised such an ignorant and misguided mother was beyond me.

I soon learned all about the evils of talc. Not to mention the wipes I was using might as well have been soaked in cyanide. "I'll send you a list of all-natural, non-toxic baby products," she said.

I know what I'm reading tonight.

Luckily, I recognized the error of my ways and purchased the approved baby items.

All was going well until…

I ordered Holland onesies that were not…

ORGANIC!

"But they have adorable duckies on them," I explained.

Quincey shook her head. "Some of these brands have dangerous chemicals in them."

I didn't order the ones made of asbestos.

Fortunately, after some research I found more acceptable material. I am proud to say Holland's clothes are made exclusively of organic lamb's wool and cloud wisps.

However, it is not just diaper products and clothing that pose a threat. Have you heard about the latest toxic toy?

The Exersaucer!

Twenty-five years ago, it was a real crowd pleaser. Basically, a swivel desk/lunch counter for babies. My girls spent a fair amount of time in that bad boy. It was a multi-tasking dream for both of us.

I've since been informed that babies should spend no more than fifteen minutes (surely, that's a misprint) a day in it.

Also, it is recommended that while in the Exersaucer, babies not stand flat-footed.

Or on their toes.

Or heels.

By process of elimination, we've placed Holland in a handstand position, and she loves it!

Relax.

It's only fifteen minutes.

But of all the atrocities I've committed in my first six months as a grandma, my lax view on television is by far the most egregious.

Apparently, the TV may have been on a couple times when Holland was over.

"It's not good for babies to watch TV before age two," Quincey said as she picked up Holland. "She's too young."

Too young to watch "The Bachelor?"

Shouldn't she learn about true love from an early age?

What about the third season of "Friends?" How is she supposed to decide if Ross and Rachel were truly on a break?

And please don't deny her "Schitt's Creek." Who else, besides Moira, can teach her the correct pronunciation of "baby."

Quincey put Holland in her highchair. She immediately started hollering and banging her teeny tiny spoon on her tray.

Quincey sighed. "She's just hungry."

Or she's upset that she won't be watching the "Bachelor" Finale.

But I didn't say anything, because…

What do I know?

Ruff Nights

My 107-year-old dog, Dixie (who barely looks a day over 98) has become sweet and mellow in her old age. This wasn't always the case. Once upon a time, Dixie was deemed a "Nuisance Dog" because she may have gotten into a kerfuffle or two. This led to a court appearance, which resulted in Animal Control mandating that Dixie wear a nuisance collar FOREVER!

(Sidenote: How about collars for "Nuisance Adults?")

The whole thing was pretty unfair because Dixie was sixteen at the time, and who among us hasn't made some poor choices in our teenage years?

The good news is that Dixie eventually grew out of her antics and matured into an upstanding canine who caused us little grief.

Until two weeks ago.

It started with Dixie waking ME (Steve was conveniently out of town) in the middle of the night. At first, it was just once a night to go to the bathroom.

I get it, Dixie. Our bladders aren't what they used to be.

But this quickly evolved into several times a night. Some nights, Dixie didn't even go to the bathroom. Instead, she would just sit on the front lawn, staring into space, deep in thought.

Dixie, you don't have any deep thoughts. YOU'RE A DOG!

Other nights, Dixie would head down the driveway, insisting on a 2 a.m. walk.

"Get back in the house!" I yelled.

But Dixie weaved and dodged as I chased her up the driveway.

I guess I was "It."

Under bushes, I scrambled. Across the lawn, I sprinted. It didn't help that it was raining. At one point, she slipped from my grasp, and I face-planted on the grass. (Highlights of this footage can be seen on our Ring video)

An hour later, I managed to coax her inside. She immediately ran to the treat bowl.

"If you think you're getting a treat for what you just did, you are sadly mistaken, Missy!" I folded my arms, so she knew who was boss!

Then I gave her a treat and we called it a night.

The following evening, my husband, Steve returned from his business trip.

"If you want something in the middle of the night," I whispered into Dixie's ear, "Daddy's your guy."

At 1:00 a.m., Dixie scratched on my side of the bed. I groaned. "We just went over this, Dixie." Then I picked her up, placed her on Steve's side, and returned to bed.

Scratch, scratch, scratch.

I elbowed Steve. "Dixie wants you."

This continued for several nights, with Dixie waking us every two hours. "It's your turn!" "No, it's your turn!" "No, I was just up, it's your turn!"

It was like having a newborn. However, at least with a newborn, that angelic face you gaze into at 2 a.m. cushions the blow.

(Dixie just read this and she is pissed!)

Dixie you, too, have the face of an angel. If I implied otherwise, I apologize.

The second week, Dixie found new ways to amuse us at 3 a.m.

Instead of roaming the front lawn, she took to roaming the hallways. With her long nails and our wood floors, it was a steady stream of clickety-clacks, like we had a tiny Clydesdale prancing through our house.

All night long, Dixie clickety-clacked from room to room in search of a bed that was *just right.*

Unfortunately, one was too hard, and one was too soft, so around 4 a.m., Dixie headed downstairs.

Click-Click-Clickety-Clack.

Both of us were wide awake and staring at the ceiling as Dixie tap danced across the kitchen tile.

"What is she doing?" Steve asked.

I sighed. "Looking for porridge?"

Dixie soon returned to our room, but instead of jumping into our bed, she burrowed beneath it. There was some initial scratching on the box spring, followed by pounding, and then what can only be described as drilling. It sounded as if Dixie was building shelves under our bed.

Can Dixie operate power tools?

I put nothing past that dog.

The next day, in a sleep-deprived stupor, I took Dixie to the vet.

"She's doing great for her age," the vet said. "But she could be experiencing some Sundowning."

The vet suggested we try either Benadryl, melatonin, or hemp.

Unfortunately, the first two didn't work, and Dixie refused to even try the hemp.

"Trust me, baby, you're going to love it," I said, holding out my hand. "All the other dogs are doing it."

Dixie walked away.

Apparently, she says *nope to the dope.*

After another sleepless week, the vet prescribed something called Trazodone, which was supposed to reduce anxiety and provide a good night's sleep.

Can I have some?

At first, Dixie wasn't interested, but when I asked, "Do you want to make it to your 114th birthday?" She changed her tune.

Now, every night around 8 p.m., I slip a pill in a piece of sweet Italian sausage, and Dixie sleeps like a pup.

No more nocturnal Dixie!

But then last week, I tried to slip her pill in a hot dog, she gave me that look.

I ordered sausage Trazodone, not hot dog Trazodone.

So, I immediately cooked her up some sausage because, let's be honest, we all know Dixie's running the show.

In fact, some might even call her the boss.

Just don't call her a nuisance.

What Happens at G'mas, Stays at G'mas

I remember when Quincey was seventeen and we went out of town for the first time.

"No friends over," I told her.

Steve was quick to add, "Especially not boys."

Boys, bad.

"And no loud music," I said.

"Don't even think about having a party, Missy." Steve folded his arms.

Quincey groaned and rolled her eyes. "It's like you don't even trust me."

Fortunately, Quincey followed the rules.

Or she didn't get caught.

That was ten years ago.

Now here we are again.

Mom and Dad were leaving for the weekend, and I don't care how old you are...

Rules are rules, Missy!

Except this time, the roles were reversed.

Quincey and her husband, Colby, were heading off to Atlanta, and her lovable, yet often misguided parents (us) were entrusted with watching 13-month-old Holland.

We sat at the kitchen table as the two of them laid down the law.

(Sidenote: It's a lot more fun to give the rules than receive the rules. Is that where the phrase, *it's better to give than receive*, comes from?)

"No TV," Quincey said.

"No Excersaucer," Colby added.

"No soaps or shampoos," Quincey said.

"Is water okay?" I asked.

Quincey nodded. "But not too hot."

"Or too cold," Colby added.

Aye-aye, Goldilocks.

"And put on *Comforting Womb Sounds* for nap time," Quincey said.

"But make sure it's not too loud," Colby added.

Steve rolled his eyes.

I may have groaned.

Parents, am I right?

The litany of rules continued.

At one point I dozed off.

When I came to, Quincey and Colby were wrapping up the Baby Bylaws with the most important rule of all…

NO SUGAR!

NOT EVEN A LITTLE!

In fact, could you please hide all items containing sugar?

We do not want Holland's pure pupils gazing upon one granule of such toxicity.

And if you think I'm exaggerating… I'm not.

When it was Holland's first birthday, all the guests enjoyed a traditional birthday cake.

Holland, however, was presented with her own single serving cake, consisting of almond flour, unsweetened cocoa powder, unsweetened applesauce, grated carrot, and non-fat Greek yogurt.

Also known as a mound of sadness.

But at G'Ma and Papa's house, we are the opposite of a mound of sadness.

We are a mound of fun.

And if we broke a few rules along the way, it's not like Holland could say anything.

God bless her limited vocabulary.

Quincey and Colby left early Saturday morning.

Saturday evening Quincey Facetimed us and I gave her a rundown of the day's events.

"And she ate all her peas…"

Smile.

"And after the park, she took a long nap…"

Smile.

"Oh, and we bought her new shoes…"

Frowny face.

"It's just that you sent her with those flimsy slipper things," I explained. "We thought she might need something sturdier."

"Please tell me you didn't buy her hard-sole shoes," Quincey said.

Sheesh, it's not like the shoes were made of cement.

Or sugar.

Quincey then proceeded to educate me on the dangers of hard-sole shoes. Phrases like "limited mobility" and "decreased dexterity" were thrown out.

"She's not wearing them now, is she?" Quincey asked, her face filled with horror.

Holland tottered past in her non-approved cinder blocks.

No, ma'am.

After that, we did our best to follow the rules.

Correction: We did our best not to get caught.

And it would have been smooth sailing if it weren't for FaceTime.

Holland's favorite thing to do is FaceTime her mom, which she did several times.

Unfortunately, she did this when the TV happened to be on.

"Sweetie, give G'Ma the phone," I whispered.

"And Papa the remote," Steve coaxed.

For a kid who isn't allowed to watch television, she sure knew her way around a remote.

"Dog-gee, Dog-gee, Dog-gee," Holland blathered into the phone while simultaneously punching the volume button.

Just a second Quince," I called, over the blaring TV.

"Why is it so loud?" Quincey yelled.

Thankfully, one of Holland's other skills is hitting the red X on the phone.

Bye, Bye.

By the time Quincey called back, we had retrieved the remote, turned off the TV, and the three of us were cuddled on the couch, reading, "Jesus Loves Me."

TV off ✓

Soft-sole shoes ✓

Biblical book: **Bonus Point.**

Quincey and Colby returned the next night.

"I told you guys had nothing to worry about," I said, as I handed her Holland's diaper bag.

"I wasn't worried," Quincey said, giving Holland a kiss on the cheek.

Then, noticing the dark brown rim around Holland's mouth, Quincey asked, "What's this?"

And that's when the two of them spotted the cup of fudge brownie gelato on the counter.

"YOU GAVE HER GELATO?" Colby clutched his heart.

Quincey had a minor stroke.

(At $8.95 a cup, we most certainly did NOT give her gelato.)

"It's black beans, I swear," I reassured them.

There was a brief 45-minute interrogation.

Fortunately, I was able to produce the empty can of beans.

They also did a thorough examination of Holland, and after concluding that she did not appear to be under the influence of sugar, they breathed a sigh of relief.

Steve and I just shook our heads.

It's like they didn't even trust us.

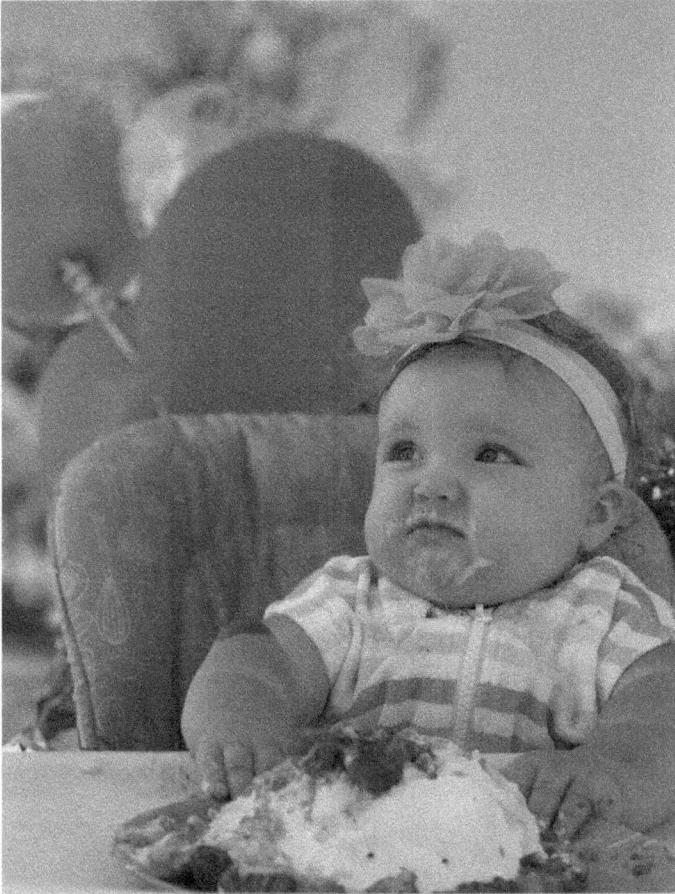

Holland's birthday wish: A real cake.

Play Nice

Years ago, it was Ms. Tanya, the preschool director, who would frequently contact us about an "incident."

These incidents usually involved our then two-year-old daughter, Quincey, gnawing on a classmate.

Ms. Tanya would sigh and hand us a paper titled ALL ABOUT MY DAY.

Where other children's papers told of toddler triumphs, ours read more like a police report:

"At 2:45 p.m., while playing in Mr. Rhino's Reading Room, Quincey bit a friend on the left cheek."

On the verge of tears, I'd apologize before Little Hannibal and I would slink out in shame.

Correction: I would slink out in shame.

Quincey would smile and wave to all her "friends."

They'd smile back, waving their freshly bitten limbs.

Such a forgiving bunch.

Fortunately, after numerous reports, calls, and special meetings, Quincey eventually grew tired of toddler flesh.

At the time, I remember thinking, *Thank God, I'll never have to go through that again.*

But here we are, twenty-five years later, and the director, Ms. Colleen, just called a meeting.

"Your dad, Don, is so social," Ms. Colleen said, as Steve and I entered her office. "I love how involved he is with all the games."

We nodded and waited for the '*But.*'

"But," Ms. Colleen sighed, "he's refusing to let people play on his Cornhole team."

An hour later, we had lunch with Don in the Belmont Senior Living Dining Room.

"Dad, you have to let everyone play," Steve explained.

"That's a stupid rule," Don grumbled. "Some of them can't even throw a beanbag." He pointed his cane at Judy, a silver-haired lady at the next table.

She glared at him over her cup of Sanka.

Clearly, bad blood between these two.

"There's a tournament with the other assisted living places," Don said. "Tony and I could win it all."

Rumor has it Tony has his own beanbags, so, Sunrise Senior Center, you've been warned.

Ms. Colleen called us several more times as tempers continued to run hot on the Over 80 Cornhole Circuit.

Don accused Bob, the young hotshot (he's 81), of using bean bags that were two ounces under regulation weight.

Bob retaliated by telling everyone that Don steps over the line when he throws.

That altercation resulted in the two of them coming to blows.

And when I say "blows," I mean they both blew angrily into their handkerchiefs.

Meanwhile, Scrabble season started last night.

Don swears it was Judy who threw the first tile.

Ms. Colleen would like to meet with us tomorrow.

It would be so much easier if they just bit each other.

Chapter 2 - In My Defense

I have no defense.

Food Truck Fiasco

Do you make yourself cringe?

Do you have regrets?

Do you often find yourself in humiliating situations brought on by your own ignorance and lack of self-awareness?

I found myself in one of these situations just last week at a concert. I was waiting in line for my order at a food truck, two brisket sandwiches with sides of coleslaw. My husband had gone to the restroom, so I struck up a conversation with the nice couple standing next to me, Jennifer and Pete. Or was it Kelly and Bob?

Having had limited experience at food trucks, I had some questions.

"How are we going to know when our order's up?" I asked, shouting over the music.

"They'll call out your name," Jennifer/Kelly said.

Jennifer/Kelly seemed to know what she was talking about, and sure enough, a minute later, I heard my name.

"January!"

That's me.

A woman walked towards me, carrying two plates of brisket sandwiches, with coleslaw on the side.

Dinner has been served.

But as she walked closer, I realized I recognized this woman.

"January, it's Susan," she said, smiling. Susan was my dental hygienist.

Hmm, this is weird. I didn't know Susan was a hygienist AND a waitress? I mean, I guess she could be both. Nobody's getting their teeth cleaned on a Saturday night. Perhaps she owns the food truck? *Good for her!*

"Nice to see you," she said, but then she started walking away.

Slow down there, Suzy, where are you going with MY brisket?

I caught up to her. "This is an awesome venue," I said.

"Definitely," she replied.

At this point, we made it to my table. "Well, here I am," I said.

Susan stopped and stared at me.

Can I have my brisket, please?

But Susan held tightly to the plastic plates.

There was a LONG pause.

"These are *my* sandwiches," Susan said.

And then the dim bulb that occupied space in my teeny, tiny brain finally turned on.

Susan was NOT the food truck waitress. Like me, Susan was a fellow concert goer and brisket sandwich connoisseur.

I took a step back.

I'm sorry, Susan, I recognize this is your brisket, not mine. You were merely calling out my name to say hello, which you now, understandably, regret.

After Susan walked away, I thought, *this is bad,* maybe not gynecologist bad, but still, you don't want the person scraping and flossing your teeth to harbor any ill will towards you.

Ten minutes later, my name was called, and I walked to the truck. A guy passed me two plates of food through the window, because as any moron knows, food trucks don't have waitresses.

Almost Taken

Last week, after getting my car detailed, we decided it was time to sell it. And when I say *we,* I mean Steve. He advertised it on Craigslist, and within minutes, the calls were pouring in. Who knew a banged-up Honda Pilot with 175,000 miles would solicit so many admirers? One such admirer was Lenny from Long Beach, who insisted on seeing it that night.

"Should I have him come here?" Steve asked.

"If you want him to murder us," I replied.

"He's not going to murder us. He just wants to buy a car."

"Don't you remember in *Taken,* when the girl's friend tells the bad guys where they live?"

Steve, not wanting to hear the entire scene, held up his hand.

A few texts later, my husband agreed to meet the murderer at the Target parking lot.

"I'll follow you there," I told him.

"Why?"

After Lenny abducts you, I'll need to describe him to the police.

24

"If you sell the car, you'll need a ride home."

"True," he said, picking up the car keys. "But don't park too close."

"You won't even know I'm there," I said. "And remember to observe any distinct features, so when he takes you, you can yell them out. Tattoo on shoulder! Scar on wrist! Unibrow!"

"What are you talking about?" he said.

Steve's limited knowledge of cinematic abductions is embarrassing.

He arranged to meet the felon at 9:00.

At 9:05, I pulled into the Target parking lot. I spotted my husband next to our car, talking with two men. That made sense. If you're going to kidnap somebody, best to have back-up.

I pulled into a space two rows over and turned off the car.

The stakeout had begun.

The younger of the two looked to be about 6 feet, bearded, and in his 30s.

The other one was a few inches shorter, bald, and around 60.

Perhaps a father/son team?

It's a shame their time is spent kidnapping innocent car-selling civilians; still, it's important to carve out family time.

The son bent down to inspect the tire, running his left hand over the rim.

Left hand? He's left-handed!

Was it too late for me to join the FBI?

Steve popped the hood and the sinister duo checked out the engine and some other stuff.

Don't ask me, I'm not a mechanic.

Steve walked away from the car.

Why was he walking away?

He pulled something out of his jacket pocket.

Oh my God, it's a GUN!

Why is he putting the gun to his ear?

Never mind, it's a phone.

He's calling the police. He's finally recognized these thugs for who they are.

My purse vibrated.

Not now people, I'm on a stakeout.

It continued to vibrate.

Steve lifted his head in my direction.

I pulled out my phone.

"I see you," I said in my best undercover voice.

"I see you too," he said. "Your lights are on."

Oh, crap!

I flipped the switch and the parking lot dimmed. No wonder I could see them so clearly.

The assassins continued to inspect the car, and a few minutes later they got into the front seat. Steve slid into the back, without yelling out one distinct character feature.

It's like he wanted to be taken.

I called him on the phone. "Where are you going?"

"For a test drive," he answered. "It's cool."

It's cool?

He never says, "*It's cool.*" Is that code for, I AM BEING TAKEN! CALL THE POLICE!

Why didn't we assign a safe word ahead of time?

What sort of FBI agent am I?

I made a mental note to come up with a really good code word for my next husband.

Lenny started the car and slowly pulled out.

Goodbye honey, I love you.

Not you, Lenny.

I waited until the car was halfway down the row before I turned on my engine.

The Pilot disappeared behind a sea of minivans. It wasn't clear which way they went.

My keen tracking skills said right, so I edged forward.

I looked right. No Pilot.

I scanned left. No Pilot.

Did they just disappear?

Is there a Platform 9¾ in the Target parking lot that I'm not aware of?

I started driving, realizing that perhaps they didn't go right or left. Maybe they went to the loading area behind Target, where it's dark and deserted and more conducive to murderous activity.

I drove slowly, looking for clues.

Nothing.

I returned to the front of the store, meandering through the food court. As I passed In-N-Out, the aroma of burgers and fries beckoned, but who could eat at a time like this?

I continued to drive up and down the rows. My stomach was in knots. I could barely finish my double-double.

Finally, I headed back to where I started, and as I prepared to turn right, a car made a left turn in front of me. It was them!

They parked, and one, two, three bodies emerged from the car, none of which were bound or gagged.

I found a spot, partially hidden, but close enough that I could see everything.

I turned off the engine AND the lights.

A good agent learns from her mistakes.

Lenny's dad hung back while Lenny and my husband talked.

Steve appeared to have all his limbs. It's like they didn't rough him up at all.

The talk escalated to an argument. Lenny gestured with his hands. My husband shook his head.

Lenny was probably saying, *I should have taken you when I had the chance.*

Steve folded his arms. *I wouldn't try it buddy, my wife is practically FBI.*

Then, a final shake of the head, and Lenny and his dad walked to their car, one row over from me.

I slid down the upholstery, holding my breath as they passed.

Miraculously, my cover wasn't blown, and my husband escaped the jaws of death.

I reminded him of this when I arrived home.

"They just wanted to buy a car," he said.

"Then, why didn't they?"

"They thought it was too much," he answered. "They were trying to low-ball me."

Low-balling sounded dangerous. I made a mental note to look it up later.

"And by the way," Steve added. "Lenny has a mole on the back of his neck."

I gave him a hug.

Maybe there's hope for him after all.

Pelotaur

She was delivered on August 24th, in the middle of our garage.

Slim, dark, about 135 pounds.

"She's beautiful," my husband Steve said, sniffling.

"I can't believe she's ours," I sighed.

And just like that, we were the proud parents of a new Peloton.

(In case you're not familiar with Peloton, it's a bike club where pretty people tell you to ride faster.)

I entered my info on the bicycle's computer screen, along with my username: BikeBender.

This was my new nickname after a slight mishap involving a bike, a pole, and myself.

We'll call it a love triangle.

My first class was a Sweat Steady Ride with Jess.

It was the equivalent of riding your bike up Mount Everest.

"For the love of God, make...it...stop!" I panted.

We were four minutes in.

Jess rode effortlessly, as she shouted out encouragement to us riders.

"SpinMonster, Happy 100th!"

Are 100-year-olds doing this ride?

"CycleQueen, Congrats on your 500th!"

Are people from the Old Testament doing this ride?

Then it dawned on me, Jess was referring to the number of rides.

500 Rides?

I just wanted to make it through one.

"Turn up that resistance!" Jess instructed.

I don't wanna.

"Increase that cadence!"

You can't make me.

"Are you bringing YOUR BEST?" Jess shouted.

I pedaled faster.

Jess smiled and sparkled like Cinderella.

I huffed and puffed like the Big Bad Wolf.

Were we doing the same class?

The good news was I eventually finished the class and I did a GREAT JOB!

Says who?

Jess.

I was invigorated and ready to start my day.

Nothing could stop me now!

Except...

I wiggled my shoes back and forth in the clips.

Uh, oh.

I pushed down on my toe, up on my heel.

Nothing.

Side to side.

Okay, new plan.

Instead of trying to get out of the clips, I would just unbuckle my shoes.

You don't need to be a rocket scientist to take off shoes.

Except these were not normal shoes.

I pushed, I pulled, I twisted.

It was like I had straightjackets on my feet.

Hey, I'm not crazy.

"Help, I'm stuck in my shoes!" I shouted to nobody.

I was in my own personal escape room.

"I'd like a hint, please," I whispered.

I tried leaning sideways, hoping that momentum would propel me out of my shoes, but no luck.

Instead, I dangled like a sweaty bat.

That was an hour ago.

So here I spin, alone in my garage, attached to my Peloton.

I'm like a centaur, but instead of half-horse, I'm half-bike.

Would that make me a Pelotaur?

I'm sure at some point, I will discover the magical button that unlocks me from these diabolical shoes.

Until then, please send help.

Preferably, a rocket scientist.

You've Got Mail

I had one stop to make on the way home, which was dropping off a book at my friend Melita's house.

What happened next was not entirely my fault.

GPS didn't tell me where her house was until I had passed it.

You had ONE job to do, GPS!

I put my car in reverse.

Boy, did I regret that.

But I can't turn back time.

I'm not Cher.

I raced backwards, passing One House, Two House...

(Red House, Blue House)

and there was her house.

Vroom!

I should have stopped.

But I didn't want to block her driveway.

It's called manners, people.

I decided to reverse a little further.

Just a smidge more, and…

THUD!

Uh, oh.

This didn't sound like my normal "Car Meets Curb."

That sound is soft and bumpy.

This was loud and crunchy.

Now before you say, "What did this crazy lady hit…this time?"

Let me assure you it was an inanimate object.

It was a mailbox.

Was is the operative word here.

The entire metal mailbox had been severed at the base of its pole.

The mangled box and pole lay helplessly on the ground.

A stump was all that remained.

I'm not going to lie.

It was shocking.

Like a mafia hitman with a vendetta against the postal service.

I stood there eying the carnage.

Do I flee the scene?

Do I send a card?

(*Where would the mailman put the card?*)

Do I place the decapitated box in their bed?

(Silly me, that's a horse head.)

Clearly, I wasn't adequately prepared on how to handle vehicular MAILSLAUGHTER.

I knocked on the door.

"So, I've got some good news and bad news," I told Alessandra and David, the daughter and son-in-law of my friend, Melita.

"Here's the book she wanted, in perfect condition," I said. "Speaking of things *not* in perfect condition…"

That's when I took them to the bloodbath.

I expected them to gasp in horror, but instead they just smiled.

"It's no big deal," Alessandra said.

"Seriously, it's not that bad," David added.

Were we looking at the same crime scene?

"EVERYONE has run into that mailbox," Alessandra said.

David nodded. "It's because the mailbox is so short."

35

Yes, blame the mailbox. I like that.

"Maybe I could take it home and fix it?" I offered.

(Says the woman who can't even sew on a button.)

"Don't worry," David reassured me. "I'll take care of it,"

Then he picked up the postal remains and headed for the house.

Alessandra and I stood there chatting next to the sad stump.

But all I kept thinking about was the poor postal worker who would be delivering the mail tomorrow.

Although, he knew the risk.

He took the oath…

"Neither rain, nor snow, nor stump…"

Fortunately, I didn't have to worry.

David had the mailbox fixed the very next day!

Forgiving and handy!

Which is ideally the type of family you want when running over their mailbox.

As for my car…

There may be some mailbox accents embedded in the bumper.

But if anybody (Steve) asks…

It was the mailbox's fault.

O Holey Night

I sat, hands clammy, trying to avoid the nine pairs of eyes that were on me. I had stalled as long as possible, but I couldn't delay the inevitable any longer.

"Your turn," someone said.

With the enthusiasm of a death row inmate, I made my way across the room.

I picked up my bag and reluctantly began handing out gifts.

Most people, when they hand out gifts, smile and say, "I hope you like it" or "I think this will be perfect for you."

I say, "I'm sorry."

Nine friends. Nine lackluster gifts. "I'm sorry, I'm sorry, I'm sorry…"

My apologies sound as if I am in Confession.

Forgive me Father, for I have shopped. And I have shopped badly.

My friends, of course, are all smiles as if they've all forgotten what a lame gift giver I am.

"I'm so excited," one of them says.

Don't be.

It's a blanket that I got on Amazon that I, too, was initially excited about because *who can't use a cozy blanket?* Marsha, from Idaho, gave it 5 stars and referred to it as "plush" and "luxurious."

But Marsha is a pathological liar because in reality, it was about as soft as a burlap sack.

Unfortunately, it was too late to return it and find something else for our annual holiday gift exchange.

But my friends don't want to hurt my feelings. "I love it," one of them said. "It keeps you warm *and* exfoliates your skin!"

I sighed.

This is how it goes every year. I just can't compete with this group of women, all of whom buy the most thoughtful gifts.

"I chose this sweater because it's made from Tibetan sheep. I had the wool dyed blue to match your eyes."

"Here's a candle that has scents of plumeria - that's your favorite, right? - and I had handprints of your granddaughter etched in the glass."

"I picked out this hummingbird feeder because I know you love hummingbirds." I ducked as something flew over my head. "Also, it comes with real hummingbirds."

But this year, I finally got smart and called for back-up. With the help of my sister-in-law, Catherine, a jewelry designer, we collaborated on the perfect gift.

And by "collaborated," I mean, Catherine said, "This is what you're getting them," and I nodded like a simpleton.

We (She) decided on beautiful, handcrafted silver keychains. Catherine etched their favorite animal in the silver disk, and attached their favorite flower on the small ring, along with their birthstone. Beautiful, classy, useful.

The keychains were scheduled to arrive on Wednesday and the party was on Saturday.

In other good news, we decided to forgo fancy holiday attire for pajamas and robes.

So, not only would I be handing out "non-sucky" gifts, I would be doing so in comfy clothes.

On Tuesday, the gifts arrived in Santa Barbara (an hour from me), which meant I would soon see those three magical words…

OUT FOR DELIVERY!

On Wednesday, they hadn't left Santa Barbara.

Hey, we all love Santa Barbara, but giddy up!

Thursday, still there.

On a positive note, I purchased Grinch pajamas.

On Friday, my keychains were finally on the move again. However, instead of "Out for Delivery," some postal genius decided to reroute them to a distribution center in Riverside, 150 miles the other direction.

If we were playing Hot-Hot-Cold, two days ago, I was warm. Now, I was cold. Oh, so cold.

"I'm sure they'll be here any minute," Steve, assured me on Saturday.

Poor naive Steve, having faith in the US Postal Service.

I arrived at the party to an assortment of beautifully wrapped gifts under the tree.

Nobody realized I hadn't brought anything, so I dropped a few subtle hints.

"You know what they say: "It's better to give than receive."

"Less is more!"

"I think friendship is probably the best gift of all!"

When it was time to exchange gifts, I took off my robe and sat down. My heart was racing, and my body felt cold, especially my left butt-cheek. *Weird.*

Once all the fabulous gifts had been dispersed, it was my turn. Nine sets of eyes turned to me. I walked to the center of the room.

"We're so excited," somebody said.

Didn't these people learn?

In fairness, I had bragged that they were going to LOVE their gifts this year.

Everyone was smiling and chattering, and the room was abuzz with holiday cheer.

That is until I started crying.

It's amazing how fast you can bring down a party if you just stand in the middle of the room and sob.

As my friends stared at me, I sniffled and explained why I had shown up at the party with big boxes of nothing.

Nobody responded. Some avoided my eyes. Others shifted uncomfortably in their seats.

I just stood, my backside freezing.

Where was that draft coming from?

That's when one of my friend's tip-toed over to me, put her hand on my shoulder and whispered, "You have a hole in your pajamas, and we can all see your butt."

She's kidding!

I put my hand on my backside, feeling around.

She's NOT kidding!

Then I looked in the hallway mirror. All of the Grinch, and Max's face…chewed to smithereens! A gaping hole was all that was left.

I knew right away it was my dog, Dixie.

Whenever I don't put away my laundry, she snacks on the nether regions of my clothes.

"We're not sure if she's a perv, or she just likes a tidy house," I told my friends.

They had additional questions.

"Does she chew on tops, or only bottoms?"

"Does she eat Steve's shorts too?"

"Do you want to put your robe back on?"

Then we all had a good chuckle and holiday cheer was restored.

I made a mental note.

Crying at party: Crowd Killer.

Mildly exposing yourself at a party: Crowd Pleaser.

Two days later, I delivered the keychains, and they were a big hit.

Of course, next year, I'll have to do this all over again, so, please, send gift ideas!

And new pajamas.

And They're Off!

This party really tested your imagination.

Last Saturday, at 3 p.m., Steve and I decided to throw a Derby party.

The Kentucky Derby started at 4, so we really needed to get moving.

The first thing you need to do when throwing a Derby party is select your horses.

The selection of the horses went quickly as Steve and I were the only two attending the party. Steve picked Angel of Empire. "I like his odds," he said.

I chose Tapit Trice. "I like alliteration."

The next thing to do when preparing for a Kentucky Derby party is to make mint juleps.

Mint juleps are the official drink of the Kentucky Derby.

The name implies that they will taste like a liquid Thin Mint.

They do not.

However, the good news is that mint juleps require only four ingredients: bourbon, simple syrup, mint, and crushed ice.

The bad news is, the main ingredient, bourbon, is gross. Unless you like drinking turpentine.

However, the simple syrup, which is basically sugar water, is delicious! (Just ask any hummingbird.) Plus, if you add enough simple syrup, you can barely taste the ~~turpentine~~ bourbon.

Some additional good news: The recipe required that I muddle the mint. More alliteration!

This party was really shaping up.

We took our mint juleps into the family room.

After setting down the drinks, I turned to Steve. "We need hats!"

I'm fairly sure *not* wearing a hat while watching the Kentucky Derby is a felony.

I'm kidding.

It's only a misdemeanor.

We ran into the laundry room and grabbed hats off the hat rack.

Mine was "beachy." His was "day laborer."

Close enough.

"Cheers!" Steve said as we clinked glasses.

He picked up the remote, and that's when we both stared at the screen.

"We may have a problem," he said.

A week earlier we had canceled our YouTube TV subscription because they were now charging $79 a month and Steve had convinced me by saying, "Seriously, when do we really need live TV?"

Um, right about now.

That's when we started scrambling. We had ten minutes to find a service that would provide live Derby action. Both of us searched and scrolled, but no luck.

Finally, I found the NBC app. "If we sign up for a free trial, we'll be able to watch it," I said.

Steve checked the time. "It's 3:57. By the time we get it, the race will be over."

Damn those fast horses!

"We could text someone for a play by play," I said.

Our friend and fellow Derby enthusiast, Bill, was thrilled to be that guy.

Well, maybe not thrilled, but he said he'd do it.

At 4:00, we got our first text. "And they're off!"

A buzz of excitement filled the room.

"I bet they're running fast!" I said.

"Really fast!" Steve said, nodding.

Then we sat in silence for a while just imagining how fast the horses were *really* going.

I checked my phone, expecting to see some live updates, like, "Tapit Trice has taken the lead," or "Angel of Empire and Tapit Trice are neck and neck."

Nothing.

"What an exciting race!" Steve said.

"A real nailbiter," I agreed.

We continued to sit, visualizing our horses racing down the stretch. This party really tested your imagination.

"Come on, Tapit Trice!" I yelled at the blank TV.

"You got this, Angel of Empire!" Steve pumped his fist at the screen of nothingness.

Thirty seconds later, our phones beeped.

One word.

"Mage."

"Is that secret horse lingo?" I asked.

Steve scanned his notes. "Nope, that's the winner."

What kind of name is Mage?!

And where was the colorful commentary and dramatic finish?

Mage is coming strongly on the outside! Angel of Empire is trying to hold him as they come down the final 16th. They're neck and neck, but it's Mage who will win the Kentucky Derby!

All we got was, "And they're off."

And two minutes later, "Mage."

I don't want to burst Bill's bubble, but I don't think he has what it takes to be a Derby announcer.

We, on the other hand, clearly had what it took to throw an amazing Derby Party. Sure, we lacked the actual seeing of the race, but our lively banter, the festive hats, and the themed cocktails more than made up for it.

Steve and I clinked our glasses in celebration, and I took a sip of the sweet turpentine.

Not bad.

Also, Sweet Turpentine would be a great name for a horse.

Chapter 3 - I Didn't Sign Up for This

You haven't experienced true trauma until you've been to a timeshare presentation.

Seminar for Sociopaths

I used to consider myself an easygoing person.

That was before my two adult daughters "temporarily" moved back in with us.

After living on their own for many years, both had gained competence, independence, and self-reliance.

Unfortunately, what they did not gain was the ability to perform basic kitchen tasks.

Don't get me wrong, they knew how to use a dish, and sometimes the dish even found its way to the dishwasher.

But the return trip to the cupboard proved problematic.

You'd think pans would reunite with pans, and bowls would find bowls, and surely spoons would rejoin fellow utensils.

YOU'D THINK?!

This is why I had no choice but to lead a kitchen organizational seminar.

"*Dish to Cupboard* Seminar starts in ten minutes," I called.

Silence.

"It's going to be fun!"

More silence.

Ten minutes later, I managed to coerce both daughters into the kitchen.

"Your dad and I will be gone for a week, and we'd appreciate you putting things where they belong," I said.

48

"We put things away," Quincey said.

I opened Exhibit A: the Tupperware cupboard.

It was a plastic battle scene, with many casualties. Orphaned lids and mismatched containers lay haphazardly throughout the shelves. A wayward measuring cup hid behind a Pyrex bowl. A wine opener had been thrown like a grenade in a popcorn bowl. It was, in all senses of the word, WILLY NILLY, and I do *not* use that phrase lightly.

I raised an eyebrow and let them soak in the carnage.

After a minute, "Well?"

Quincey shrugged.

"Looks good to me," Parker said.

Had I raised sociopaths?

I took a deep breath. "Each container has a matching lid, and they should stay together. They're a pair, like socks."

I looked down at my daughters' feet. Both were wearing mismatched socks.

Good God, they WERE sociopaths.

(Also, mental note: Plan sock seminar.)

"Fine, we get it," Parker said. "Are we done yet?"

"See these dishes?" I pointed to the array of pots and pans lying next to the sink. "They're not nomads, they have homes."

"They were drying," Quincey said.

"For a week?" I handed her a frying pan.

I passed Parker a casserole dish.

"Why don't you put these away," I instructed.

"I thought this was more of an informational seminar," Quincey said.

Parker nodded. "Like the history of dishes."

I sighed.

"Come on, I believe in you two," I said.

I didn't, but best to keep it positive.

Which wasn't easy since I felt like I was leading a painful game of *Hot and Cold*.

"Warm, warmer...no, colder...nope, pots don't go in the oven."

It was like watching two blind mice.

"Still cold...okay, a little warmer," I said to Quincey, as she began edging towards the pots and pans cupboard. "Getting hotter!"

Meanwhile Parker had meandered into the living room and was watching *Ozark*.

"Cold, Parker, very cold!" I called.

Parker rolled her eyes and returned to the kitchen.

An eternity later, I finally shouted, "Hot! You are on fire!" as the last dish was returned to the cupboard.

"Okay, this is the last thing we're going to go over," I said, pointing to the clean/dirty magnetic sign on the dishwasher.

"It's pretty simple, when the sign says dirty..."

But it was too late. Both had escaped. Seminar over.

A shame too because the dishwasher sign demonstration was sure to be a crowd pleaser.

I shook my head.

Games, visuals, hands-on demonstrations…what more could I have provided?

Then, suddenly, I realized what had been missing all along…

And what would liven up tomorrow's "Plants Need Water" seminar…

Alcohol.

I told you I was easygoing.

The Maximalist

Back in March, I led a workshop entitled, Seminar for Sociopaths. It was widely popular.

Two out of the three participants stayed until the very end.

I taught the importance of reuniting Tupperware containers with their significant lids.

Nine months later, it was time for a new seminar, except this time my daughter, Parker, would be the teacher and I would be the pupil.

Like so many millennials, Parker has been heavily influenced by a certain movement.

Communism?

Socialism?

Veganism?

Worse.

Minimalism.

This is a popular movement, recently inspired by Joshua Milburn and Ryan Nicodemus. These two young men threw away all their crap, found perspective, and now lead more meaningful lives.

Can't I have a meaningful life with my crap?

The Seminar started at 8 a.m. sharp.

Apparently, minimalists are tidy *and* prompt.

"I made coffee," Parker said.

How sweet.

I opened my cupboard, revealing a parking garage of coffee mugs.

"You have forty-three mugs," Parker said, over my shoulder.

Not sweet! Entrapment!

"Well, it's just that…"

She opened another cabinet. "And twenty-two bowls."

"But, hey," I said, "If two soccer teams show up, Frosted Flakes for everybody!"

She rolled her eyes, clearly not amused.

Can I have a different instructor?

Parker opened the oven, revealing an assortment of cookie sheets. "And why are these in the oven?"

"Overflow," I said.

She tsked.

The chances of me passing this workshop were slim.

"Here's the problem," she said, opening the cupboard next to the oven.

In a matter of minutes, a plethora of kitchen appliances were strewn across the tile floor.

I was asked to identify and explain each one.

It was like a crime scene, but less fun.

"A waffle maker?" She raised an eyebrow.

"I used to make waffles," I insisted.

"When?"

"Early 2000s," I admitted.

She held up an unrecognizable yellow apparatus. "Do you know what this is?"

"Uh, I'm not sure..." I stammered, wiping sweat from my forehead.

"It's a donut machine," she said. "Have you *ever* made donuts?"

"No, ma'am."

The waffle iron and donut maker were thrown into a cardboard box.

"I'm kind of thirsty. Maybe I could get a drink of water?" I asked.

"Sure, which of the forty-three mugs would you like to use?" she said.

Man, I walked right into that one.

She pulled out an enormous baggie of plastic curly straws. "And would you like a straw with your water?"

Yes, please.

She shook her head.

I mean, no, thank you.

"I didn't get rid of the straws because they're not biodegradable," I explained.

Let the record show I was saving the environment.

Parker was not impressed. She was too busy removing, classifying, and interrogating. She continued to pepper me with questions. At times, I tried to infuse humor, but she wasn't having it. I kept hoping Good Cop would show up, but no such luck. Parker was two Bad Cops rolled into one.

Finally, we were down to our last item.

A gigantic black spaceship-looking contraption with a red cover was placed in the center of the room.

"What is this?"

Well, there's a blast from the past!

"It's a wok," I explained. "When your dad and I first got married, we were really into Chinese stir fry."

"Thirty years ago," she said.

I nodded.

"And will you be using it any time soon?"

"Maybe…"

"Chinese food gives you heartburn, the handle is missing, and the cord looks like an electrical hazard."

Officer Parker was really making some solid points.

She threw the wok in the cardboard box.

"We're all done," she said.

Within minutes, boxes were sealed, taped, and put into the back of her vehicle to be transported.

To where?

Who knew?

All I knew was that congestion and clutter had been replaced with wide open space.

In less than an hour, I had gone from a maximalist to a minimalist.

And even better news, I had been paroled.

"Meet me in the garage in an hour," Parker said, exiting the kitchen.

I guess I was still on probation.

AirbnBAD

Do you know who the best people in the world are?

Nuns? Buddhist monks? Trader Joe's employees?

Airbnb hosts. These gracious people rent out their homes to tourists, welcoming us with open arms and bottles of wine. They inform us of the sights we simply must see. They promptly respond to any questions or concerns we may have. By the end of the visit, we are like family.

"Arrivederci, my Italian sister!"

"Au Revoir, my French brother!"

I've never met an Airbnb host I didn't like.

Then I met Marlene. Marlene was bad news from the get-go.

After a long day of travel, my husband, Steve, Parker, and I arrived at Marlene's place in Salzburg. It was after 9 p.m. and all the grocery stores were closed. However, Marlene had mentioned that welcome drinks would be waiting for us. After we settled in, we went in search of the refreshing beverages we had been promised.

I scanned the counter. *Nothing.*

Parker opened the fridge. *Empty.*

My husband looked in the freezer. *Nein.*

Did she hide them?

Hey, I'm all for scavenger hunts but a clue would be nice.

After texting Marlene about the welcome drinks, she responded, "I'll drop them off tomorrow." Then she added, "Don't forget to look over the binder."

56

The binder was a notebook, titled "HOUSE RULES," and rivaled the length of the Bible.

This mandated house orientation covered everything from opening the balcony door: ONLY TURN KNOB ¼ ROTATION AND PULL VERY GENTLY OR YOU COULD DAMAGE DOOR to bathroom shower etiquette: OPEN BATHROOM WINDOWS IMMEDIATELY FOLLOWING A SHOWER!

Around the time we got to the Excessive Noise Chapter: NO LOUD NOISE EVER! I whispered to Steve, "I need fresh air."

I headed to the balcony and just as I was about to turn the knob, my hand froze.

Was it a ¼ turn or ½ turn? Do I push or do I pull?

I returned to the couch, next to my dozing daughter, and elbowed her awake.

"Only use pods in the washing machine," she mumbled.

Marlene's manifesto finally concluded with: FAILURE TO LEAVE KEYS IN DESIGNATED LOCK BOX WILL RESULT IN FINES!

Exhausted from orientation and dehydrated from lack of welcome drinks, we went to bed.

Marlene stopped by the next morning, handing us two beers. There were three of us.

Did one of us not look thirsty?

After chatting for a few minutes, Marlene said. "Well, I better get back to work,"

"What do you do?" I asked, thinking she was a shop owner. For some reason, I assume everybody in Europe owns a shop.

"I'm a doctor," she said.

My husband and I looked at each other. Here we were complaining about welcome drinks and manifestos when Doctor Marlene was busy saving lives. Right now, there's probably a guy (we'll call him Bob) waiting for a kidney. And because of us, he has to wait a little longer.

Run, Marlene, run! Get Bob that kidney!

"What kind of doctor?" my husband asked.

"A podiatrist."

Bob can wait.

"So, I noticed in the binder that we need to mop after we shower," I said.

She nodded. "It's no big deal, just some light mopping."

I love when my Airbnb comes with chores.

After Marlene left, we decided to have coffee. Marlene had left so many pods we could have coffee several times a day if we wanted, except for one problem...

The oval coffee pod was bigger than its designated oval home. We texted Marlene that she had given us the wrong pods. Marlene responded with a video on how to operate your coffee machine.

Hey, Doctor, we may not be able to remove bunions, but I'm fairly sure we know how to make coffee.

Marlene promised to stop by later and take a look. Sadly, her promises were as empty as our coffee cups.

However, Marlene's empty promises didn't even come close to the true horror we were about to encounter...

Mopping.

And not just any mopping… naked mopping!

What kind of story is this?

Thankfully, one without pictures.

Allow me to explain about what Marlene had casually referred to as "no big deal" and "some light mopping."

Marlene, you pathological liar.

As stated in the binder, following each shower, GUESTS MUST MOP UP EXCESS WATER!

Isn't the shower door responsible for keeping water in, so post-shower mopping is NOT required? That's one of the perks of the shower door.

Unfortunately, Marlene's diabolical shower door was designed to cover only half the shower area. In addition, there was no metal track to stop water from seeping out. However, the real kicker was that the bathroom was built on a slant so that water drained away from the shower. This resulted in Marlene's bathroom becoming a wading pool after each shower.

We had a family meeting to discuss our options. Not showering seemed like the safest bet, but in the end, hygiene won. We decided to take extremely efficient showers, which went something like this:

Turn on shower.

FREEZING!

Shampoo head. Lather, scrub, lather.

Uh, oh, water is trickling past the shower door.

Lather, scrub, lather, faster, faster, faster!

Trickle has turned into a stream.

Shut off water. Jump out of shower. (Don't actually jump, it's slippery.)

Retrieve broom, divert water back into shower.

You missed a puddle.

Mop, mop, mop!

Mop like nobody's watching!

Return broom to designated spot.

Turn water back on.

Holy Binder, it's still cold!

Remember, freezing water is proven to reduce stress. Don't you feel relaxed?

Conditioner on hair, soap on body.

Scrub, scrub, scrub! Clean, clean, clean!

Water rising, racing towards cupboards!

Abort washing, turn off shower.

Grab broom, mop, mop, mop!

Good God, Woman, is that the best you can do? Put your legs into it. Squat and Mop!

Ignore conditioner running into eyes. Mop with eyes closed!

Blind naked mopping! Did I just invent a sport?

Return broom.

Turn shower back on, monitor water level with non-soapy eye…

And so, our week at Marlene's continued…so much mopping, so little coffee.

We finally heard from Marlene the day we checked out, informing us to LEAVE KEYS IN DESIGNATED LOCKBOX OR WE WOULD BE FINED!

She also reminded us to write a review.

I don't think that will be a problem.

Confessions of a Plantaholic

It started innocently enough: A hibiscus here, a geranium there.

Then came the roses, the lantanas, the birds of paradise.

Don't even get me started on succulents!

My family thinks I may have a problem.

Sure, I spend a lot of time talking about my plants.

Or talking to my plants.

Or talking to my plants about other plants.

But I don't have a problem.

Before heading out of town recently, I asked the kids, "So, who wants to take care of my babies?"

Wow, Parker and Colby can really move!

Quincey, now in her third trimester, wasn't as nimble.

"I just don't have an extra four hours a day," she said.

Psh. It's like three hours, tops.

I returned to packing.

Purse: ☑

Make-up: ☑

Bag of succulents: ☑

Yep, nothing weird here.

Last week was Mother's Day and Quincey bought me a subscription to a Succulent of the Month club.

This club kicks "Jelly of the Month Club's" ass!

When my first succulent arrived, I tore open the box and discovered a petite, yet perky little guy named Dedos (Sedum Pachyphyllum, when he's feeling formal).

"Isn't this exciting?" I asked Steve.

His response: "Don't you think you have enough plants?"

YOU CAN NEVER HAVE ENOUGH PLANTS!

Also, I don't have a problem.

Fortunately, there's one person that shares my affinity for horticulture: My mom.

Like me, she's a plant ~~enabler~~ enthusiast.

Besides discussing plants, we both enjoy exploring our local nursery.

The amount of time I spend there is staggering. On more than one occasion, I've been mistaken as an employee…

by an employee.

Is it because I occasionally throw on an apron and lead a workshop on drought resistant foliage?

Who can say?

I think what my family is most concerned about is the time I spend in my garden, not planting, not weeding, just staring.

It wasn't long ago that my friend Kim told me how her husband loves to stand in their backyard and stare at their fruit trees. At the time, I replied, "That's weird."

But look at me now...

Standing in my garden, just me, a shovel, and a whole lot of plants.

Except…

I wasn't by myself.

Right behind me, seated in a semicircle, was my family.

Well, look who's excited about today's home garden tour!

I dove right in, starting with the origin of the plant (Portugal), and then peppered them with questions. "Does anybody know how much sun an oleander needs?"

Not one hand shot up.

Tough crowd.

They all looked at one another.

Steve gave Parker a nod.

Parker picked up the shovel.

Are they going to bury me alive?

Tough intervention.

My husband tapped the seat next to him. "Honey, it's time to walk away from the Portuguese plant."

He WAS paying attention!

Also…

I may have a problem.

The Price of Paradise

Steve, and I were recently involved in a hostage situation.

It didn't involve guns or terrorists.

It did, however, involve intimidation tactics, guilt, and mind games.

Tom, our captor, led us down a hallway to a small room.

He gave us water.

Sparkling water because we were high-end hostages.

Tom told us to sit down.

In a little bit, he'd be taking us somewhere else, but for now, he just wanted to get to know us.

Tom didn't want to hurt us.

Tom wanted the best for us.

Tom wanted to sell us a timeshare.

Of course, we had no intention of buying, as we told the salesperson who first contacted us.

"I think you'll change your mind when you see what we have to offer," the salesperson replied.

Then he offered us four nights at a beautiful Hawaiian resort, with the agreement that we attend a two-hour timeshare presentation.

But timeshare hours do not move at a normal pace.

One timeshare hour = one gazillion regular hours.

Before the presentation, Steve and I roleplayed different scenarios and practiced our assertive NOs!

"No means NO!" I shouted.

"Maybe a little less crazy," Steve said.

"We're not interested," I stated firmly.

Steve gave me the thumbs up.

"And don't forget," Steve added. "The salesperson is going to try and connect with whichever one of us he thinks is the weakest link."

Steve and I both pointed at each other and then spent the next twenty minutes arguing over who was the weakest link.

We weren't off to a great start.

Ten minutes into the presentation, Tom turned to me and said, "January, I can tell this location is going to be perfect for you."

Steve coughed, *Weakest link.*

We headed over to the two-bedroom unit that Tom thought would be ideal for our family. Taking a seat at the kitchen table, Tom pointed to one bedroom. "Now, January, that's the master for you and Steve." He then pointed to the other room. "And this one would be perfect for Quincey and Colby."

I gave him my children's names?

Please don't tell Quincey.

"It's a nice timeshare," I said.

"January, this is not a timeshare, this is VACATION OWNERSHIP," Tom stated. "There's a big difference."

Then he went on to *not* explain the difference, but he did continue to use my name in every sentence.

Did Tom think I didn't know my own name?

As he spoke, Tom locked eyes with mine with such intensity that I couldn't look away.

Was Tom a Timeshare Wizard?

"January, you know who's really going to enjoy this place," Tom said, pausing dramatically. "Holland!"

I told him about my granddaughter?

Definitely don't tell Quincey.

"We have an amazing pool," Tom said. "Holland is going to love the waterslide!"

"She's only fifteen months," Steve said.

"Seventeen months," Tom and I both corrected him.

I looked at my watch.

Just one gazillion hours to go.

Tom walked us back to the main office. "January, this really is an unbelievable opportunity," he said. "*Everyone* who has come in today has bought a place!"

Not everyone, Tom.

"Why don't we go look at some numbers." He led us down a series of stairways and through a maze of intricate halls.

Tom was taking us to the cavernous depths of ~~timeshare~~ vacation ownership Hell.

Steve and I took a seat in the office. Tom pointed to the people on his computer enjoying their luxurious vacations and added that we were "just a signature away!"

Steve and I shared a sideways glance.

Tom didn't intimidate us.

Sure, he was tall and most likely a wizard, but it was two vs one.

But there was no way he was going to talk us into buying.

Then the door opened…

A tall, aggressively beautiful woman appeared.

She took Tom's chair. Tom took a seat in the corner.

Was Tom in trouble?

The woman introduced herself as Fiona (no relationship to Shrek) and gave us a bone-chilling smile.

Fiona had the air of Cruella de Vil, but without the fur.

Or puppies.

(Sidenote: I could use an emotional support puppy right now.)

"January and Steve, I'm sure Tom told you how quickly these units are selling, and we don't want you to miss out," Fiona said.

She whipped out a notepad and began scribbling a series of numbers, many of which she circled and underlined at a ferocious pace, like some deranged accountant.

"You can pay the full amount (Circle!), or we can do a payment plan (Underline!), and let's not forget about all the bonus points (Two circles and an arrow!)."

"Thank you, but we're going to pass," Steve said.

Fiona didn't miss a beat.

At a rapid-fire pace, she threw out names of other places where we could own. "The Big Island! Oahu! Orlando!"

"Holland will love the waterslide there," Tom interjected.

(Hey, Buddy, Holland can't even swim, so stop sending her down the waterslide.)

"And if you go in May or October, it'll cost you less points," Fiona said.

"Of course, you'll have to take Holland out of school," Tom said.

Now Holland's a truant.

Thanks a lot, Tom.

"I don't think so," Steve said.

"However, for a much lower price, you can just purchase points that give you access to our amazing hotels all over the world." Fiona wrote down another number.

I looked at my watch.

Two gazillion hours were finally up!

I turned to Steve, *We're free!*

But Steve was looking at the number. "Hmm," he said.

Fiona smiled. Tom leaned forward.

Like sharks, they smelled blood.

Steve looked at me.

Maybe?

I glared back.

Are you insane?

Fiona handed Steve a pen, but before she could get his signature, I said, "Hon, you're retiring soon, so this wouldn't be a good idea."

"We're not interested," I told Fiona.

Ignoring me, Fiona started writing again, "I shouldn't even do this but I'm going to offer you EVEN MORE POINTS (Circle! Circle! Underline! Arrow! Arrow! Arrow!) …"

Tom was still yelling about waterslides.

The room was spinning.

I was on the verge of a timeshare-induced panic attack.

I stood up and hollered, "NO MEANS NO!"

The room became quiet.

Fiona stopped writing. She pursed her lips. "Okay, then."

What followed was a long awkward silence.

After that, Fiona let us know that although they weren't angry with us, they were disappointed. She also said she hoped we wouldn't regret this decision. But we probably would.

Before handing us our timeshare detention sheet Fiona said, "Just like Darryl."

Tom nodded. "Poor Darryl."

The two of them looked to the Heavens.

Oh, God. Did they kill Darryl?

Are they going to kill us too and bury our bodies in the spacious two-bedroom with the partial ocean view?

"Darryl had an opportunity to buy a prime ocean view unit in 2017, but he didn't," Fiona explained, her eyes boring into mine. "Now all he can afford is a garden view at the Best Western."

Hallelujah, he's alive!

Reluctantly Fiona handed over the pen.

The Weakest Link and I frantically signed our Timeshare Detention Sheet.

Tom walked us down the hall.

He wasn't as chatty as earlier.

Steve and I stared straight ahead, our hearts pounding. I had visions of Fiona finding a loophole in the contract, chasing us down, and making us return for another presentation.

It wasn't until we opened the exit door, and warm air touched my cheek, did I finally breathe.

Tom called out, "Have a good day!"

Or was it…

"YOU'LL RUE THE DAY!"

Post-timeshare jumping for joy. (My vertical leap isn't what it once was.)

Chapter 4 - That Guy

"I love you more than an air-conditioned house." - Me

"I love you more than a Costco hot dog." – Steve

Those Five Words

There are five words that my husband has said to me every day for the last thirty years.

"You're the most beautiful woman."

So close.

His five-word phrase is far deeper than superficial compliments. These words embody the depth of my husband's soul, his core values, and his reason for living.

"Have you thought of dinner?"

It's quite impressive that he's managed to ask the same question for 10,950 consecutive days.

It's also a little insulting.

Hey, Buddy, maybe instead of pondering pork chops, I was mentally solving trade relations with China.

I wasn't.

But I could have been.

Usually, he poses the question around 3:00 in the afternoon. "Have you thought of dinner?"

Not even a little.

It's not that I'm opposed to making dinner. I have the time and I enjoy cooking.

It's just must we have dinner every night?

Like neighborhood stop signs, can't it be optional?

I say 5/7 nights is plenty.

That's a solid 71%. Not honor roll, but getting the job done.

And what defines dinner?

Sometimes I'll make an elaborate cheese plate. I fill the platter with an assortment of meats, cheeses, fruits, and crackers. It's got your four basic food groups so I think we can all agree, THIS IS YOUR DINNER!

"Delicious," Steve said, polishing off his weight in Gouda. "So, what's for dinner?"

I'm tempted to remove his limbs with cheese tongs.

But why ruin perfectly good tongs?

You'd think I'd get a reprieve from this question, but his consistency is unwavering.

He can be on a business trip 3,000 miles away, and still, he'll want to know my deep and profound thoughts on this all-important meal.

"You're not even here," I answered.

"I was just wondering what *you* were having for dinner."

Like a dedicated postal worker, neither rain, nor sleet, nor surgical procedure can deter him.

"Have you thought of dinner?" He asked a couple of nights ago.

"You're having a colonoscopy tomorrow," I answered.

"So?"

"So, Jell-O," I said.

"And?"

"Broth."

"And?"

"Magnesium citrate," I answered.

"That doesn't sound like a real meal."

"It's not," I said.

He sighed. Clearly the idea of a liquid dinner had cut him to the core.

"But we're having something special tomorrow night," I added.

His eyes grew wide, and his expression turned to pure joy. He spoke slowly, "You've already thought of tomorrow night's dinner?"

No, but I acknowledged there would be dinner tomorrow night.

He gave me a hug. "Thanks hon, you're the best!"

I smiled.

It's the thought that counts.

And those are my five words.

Hot Diggity Dog

Steve loves a good dog.

The four-legged kind that goes, "Ruff?"

Yes, those too.

But the dogs I'm talking about are a quarter pound of select beef and served at your local Costco.

Steve loves a Costco hotdog.

Perhaps, too much.

Last year, he was convinced there was fraudulent activity on his credit card when he noticed the Costco Food Court charges.

"I think somebody stole my card and bought a lot of hotdogs," he said.

"You have relish on your shirt," I said.

Soon after, Steve finally accepted that he might be over-indulging.

However, not wanting to give them up completely, he did what any sane person would do.

He began tracking his hotdogs.

But then, who doesn't?

We discovered this a few months ago during a family Costco trip. We had just finished shopping and we were all hungry.

"Let's get hot dogs," Quincey suggested.

Steve's face lit up and he got a dreamy, lovesick look in his eyes, like the way he used to look at me.

I'm joking.

He still looks at me that way.

If I'm holding a hot dog.

He immediately took out a small notebook and recorded something.

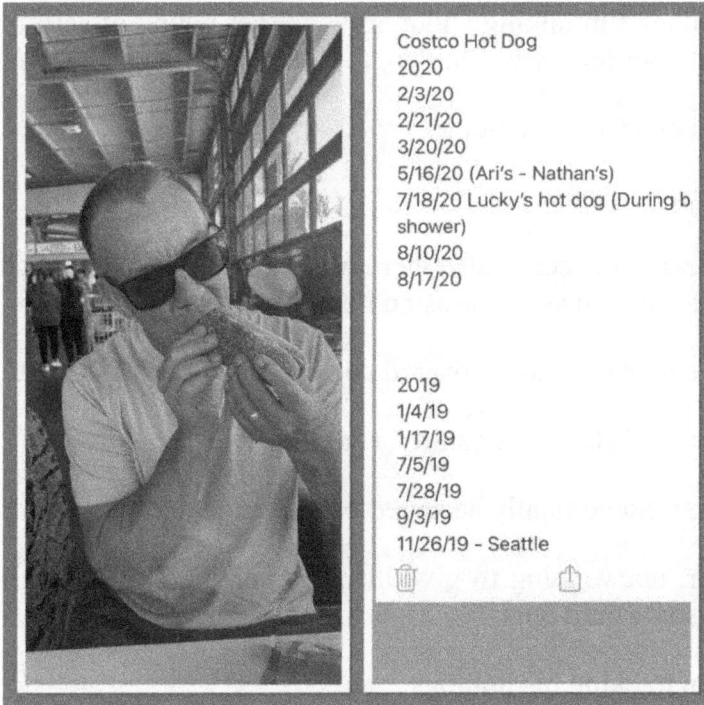

Costco Hot Dog
2020
2/3/20
2/21/20
3/20/20
5/16/20 (Ari's - Nathan's)
7/18/20 Lucky's hot dog (During b shower)
8/10/20
8/17/20

2019
1/4/19
1/17/19
7/5/19
7/28/19
9/3/19
11/26/19 - Seattle

The log is no joke.

"What are you doing?" our daughter, Parker, asked.

"Updating my hotdog log,'" he said, and then went on to explain it.

Basically, it's like your kid's elementary school reading log. The kid records how many minutes he or she reads, and the parent signs it.

Steve records every hot dog he eats.

However, I don't have to sign it.

At least I don't think I do.

There were a lot of questions.

"How many dogs a year?" "What if you exceed your quota?" "What if you lose your notebook?"

"Twelve." "I HAVE SELF-CONTROL!" "It's backed up on an excel spreadsheet."

That was April.

In mid-May he was one under his annual hotdog quota (Good job, Steve!).

During this time, we celebrated our goddaughter's graduation at a family barbeque.

Guess what they were serving?

I'll give you a hint: it was filled with nitrates.

As the dogs sizzled on the grill, Steve took out his notebook and entered the required information.

He had just explained to the other guests how the hotdog log worked. They smiled, nodded politely, and all pretended that a hotdog log was perfectly normal.

A few minutes later Steve looked up in anticipation as lunch was served.

Hello, Gorgeous!

But uh oh…

This wasn't a COSTCO hotdog.

To put it in real dog terms: A Costco hotdog is a Great Dane.

This hotdog was a chihuahua.

A delicious chihuahua, but a chihuahua, nonetheless.

"If it's not a Costco hotdog, it shouldn't count," I told him.

Steve hung his head. "I've already entered it."

We all tried to convince him that it would be okay to change it, but he wouldn't waver.

Geez, it's not like it was written in blood...

or ketchup.

But what can I say, the guy's got ethics.

Papa! Papa! Papa!

My eighteen-month-old granddaughter, Holland, toddled through our front door, squealing with delight.

"Holland!" I yelled, running into the entryway.

Her eyes were huge with excitement.

My arms were wide open.

Her arms were wide open.

"Holland!" I rushed towards her.

She gurgled with glee, arms outstretched.

It was like a scene out of a movie: Two people, so overcome with love, that they can't wait to fall into each other's embrace.

I got down on my knees and waited for Holland's little arms to wrap around me.

"Papa!" Holland screamed in delight, giving me a gentle, yet firm push out of the way.

I tumbled to the floor, Holland raced past me, and fell into the arms of the one and only...

PAPA!

(My husband, Steve)

It's all about Papa...

Papa! Papa! Papa!

As Holland squeezed Papa, she gave me a courtesy wave.

Now, don't get me wrong, Holland loves me.

The two of us have a wonderful time building blocks, reading books, blowing bubbles.

But often in the midst of us playing, Holland will get a faraway look in her eyes, as if in a trance, and whisper...

"Papa."

I'm convinced that the quieter Holland whispers your name, the more she loves you.

"Papa," Holland purrs.

Sometimes she just mouths, "Papa," as if the word was too sacred to utter aloud.

I don't get it.

Sure, he's a great guy, but have you met me?

I'm a ton of fun.

"Holland, you know I'm not like a regular grandma," I reminded her. "I'm a cool grandma."

She smiled.

"Papa," she whispered.

"Ma," I say. "Can you say Ma?"

"Papa," she babbled.

"Ma," I instruct.

This can go on for a while.

Sometimes she surprises me and throws in a "Dixie."

Dixie is our dog.

So just to review, it's Papa for the Gold and Dixie takes the Silver.

I'd like to think I'm still on the podium.

But, seriously, what's the deal with Papa?

My theory is that Papa is bribing her with non-approved sugary snacks when no one is looking.

Not cool, Papa.

"I'm not going to stoop to that," I told Holland, shaking my head and slipping her a Snickers.

When her mom picked her up, she eyed Holland suspiciously.

"Who gave her chocolate?"

Steve and I both answered, "Not me."

Holland smiled, a faint dark ring around her mouth.

"MAAAAA!" Holland bellowed.

Now you say my name.

Although, it's not quite the angelic tone she uses for Papa's name.

It's more like the screeching wail of a macaw parrot.

"MAAAAAA!" she hollered again, ratting me out.

Then she ran to me and wrapped her arms around me.

Totally worth it.

"I love you, Holland," I whispered to her.

She whispered back…

"Papa."

Too Many Cooks in the Kayak

Steve and I went kayaking last year.

For those of you considering kayaking with your spouse, let me just say…

Don't do it!

(Like a Nike ad, but the opposite)

In fact, why don't I just save you the trouble and paint you a picture of how your day will go.

The arguing will begin three seconds after you get in the boat because you will both assume you are the captain.

Obviously, the captain is the one who is the first to say, "I Am Your Captain Now!"

That's just maritime law.

Some people (Steve!) won't follow these rules and will try to convince you the captain is the person seated in the back of the kayak.

You'll debate ship protocol before finally agreeing that nobody gets to be captain. Then you'll make up snarky names for each other like, *Captain Sassy, Captain Corrector, Captain "Do You Even Know What You're Doing?"*

While you're insulting each other, there will be a big splash in the water, and nearby kayakers will holler, "WHALE!"

Seeing humpback whales was the whole reason you decided to kayak, and now you've missed them.

Allow ten minutes to argue over whose fault that was.

Also, you've been drifting aimlessly so you better use those oars.

Left, right, left, right…

Marital bliss is restored as you paddle in sync.

"Good job!"

"You too!"

Awe, love on the high seas!

But the current is pulling you to the right so…

Left, left, left.

"What are you doing?"

"I'm straightening us out because the current is taking us out *that* way."

"No, the current is going *that* way."

"It *was* going *that* way, but it changed."

"Currents don't change that quickly."

This will be followed by an in-depth lesson on currents, and you'll think to yourself, *I didn't know I married Bill Nye, the Science Guy.*

Meanwhile, there's an even bigger splash in the water, followed by squeals of joy. "DID YOU SEE THAT TAIL?!"

No, you did not because you were busy learning about the earth's gravitational pull.

Back to rowing…

Left, right, left, right…

Other kayakers glide by, smiling.

(They're obviously not married.)

"See how they're in sync because she's listening to him?"

"See how he's not bossing her around?"

Both of you will then simultaneously daydream about the other falling overboard and being swallowed by a whale.

But not in a mean, murdery way.

More like a "Go sit in the belly of the whale and think about your actions" way.

Now that your hour is almost up, it's time to head back.

Left, right, left, right…

Paddling against the current, your arms will be aching, and you don't seem to be getting anywhere.

And that's when you'll see it.

On the horizon, a whale will launch his entire body out of the water, momentarily suspended in air.

"BREECH!" You'll both shriek, gazing in awe and smiling at one another.

"I'm sorry I wished for a whale to swallow you whole," you'll say to one another.

Left, right, left, right…

A few minutes later, the instructor will signal you in.

Unfortunately, one of you will paddle right when it should be left.

"It's always left, right, left!"

"Why can't it be right, left, right?"

A mutiny will ensue, the kayak will tilt sideways, and a wave will capsize the vessel.

Soaking wet, and dragging the kayak to shore, you swear you'll never do that again!

86

But kayaking is like childbirth. The painful memory will fade and somehow, you'll convince yourself it wasn't that bad.

Which is why this past February you could find Steve and me, once again, heading over to the kayak rentals.

However, we're not complete morons.

When the instructor asked, "Single or double?"

We both answered, "Single!"

Those Four Words

Steve, used to utter his famous catchphrase "Have you thought of dinner?" about thirty times a day. The first few times he'd ask, I'd nod, with a faraway look in my eyes, as if gourmet meals were dancing in my head.

By the 20th time, I wasn't nodding anymore, and the look was less faraway, and more murdery.

For thirty years, this was our routine.

Then a few months ago, I broke my ankle, and everything changed. Now that I was no longer mobile, Steve was quickly promoted to Top Chef.

Congrats, Buddy.

"Have you thought of dinner?" I'd call from the couch.

"We're having chicken thighs, brown rice, and a Greek salad," Steve answered.

Apparently, he had.

For three straight months, Steve prepared and served delicious meals.

Not going to lie, I contemplated smashing my other ankle.

But now that I'm out of my boot, and finally mobile, I was reinstated as Top Chef. (I did not vote for myself.)

A few weeks ago, Steve sauntered into the kitchen around 4:00, which is prime time "thinking about dinner time."

I braced myself for the inevitable five words.

They never came.

Instead, he shook his head at the container of feta and said, "I'm on Whole 30."

For those of you not familiar with Whole 30, it's a nutritional plan with strict guidelines.

In literary terms, what you *can* eat is equivalent to a sad haiku:

> Fruit, veggies, seafood,

> Unprocessed meats, seeds, and nuts,

> Black coffee, yum, yum.

The list of what you *can't* eat is comparable to *The Odyssey*.

To make matters worse, Quincey and Colby were doing Whole 30 with Steve. When the three of them got together, all they did was talk about how great they felt. Then, they'd eat gross food and pretend it was good.

"Delicious," Quincey said, munching on roasted kale.

Steve took a bite and nodded. "It tastes like French fries."

Kale (roasted or otherwise) does NOT taste like French fries!

You know what does taste like french fries?

FRENCH FRIES!

As if leafy greens and positive attitudes weren't bad enough…

Steve was losing weight and telling me about it.

"Honey, I've lost seven pounds," he called, as he stepped off the scale, smiling.

"And it's only been a week."

For the record, the last time I lost even close to seven pounds was because a baby was removed from my body.

But really, I'm happy for him.

"It's because I'm doing Whole 30," he explained.

Steve thinks the more one talks about Whole 30, the more weight one loses.

He may be on to something.

Two weeks in, Steve was down ten pounds and feeling great. Not surprising since Whole 30 promised increased energy, better sleep, improved digestion, blah, blah, blah.

"You know," he said, "this is the first time in my life I've ever dieted. It's kind of fun."

I wanted to bludgeon him with the bathroom scale, but since I wasn't on Whole 30, I didn't have the energy.

Last week, while out on a walk, we ran into some neighbors.

"How are you guys doing?" they asked.

"Great," Steve smiled. "I'm on Whole 30."

I gave the neighbor a, *sorry my husband hates added sugars* look.

But the neighbor replied, "I love Whole 30."

Then they talked about sweet potatoes.

Spoiler alert: They can be used as a Whole 30 dessert!

But here's the good news…

It's been almost 30 days.

Steve talked about extending his Whole 30 another month, but I reminded him it's not Whole 60. *Enough is enough, Buddy.*

It's time to enjoy a Costco hotdog and ask me if I've thought of dinner.

Some Like It Hot

I've heard stories of people who live in houses and, when the temperature gets too hot, a magical box turns on, and a stream of cool air fills the house and the husband and wife live happily ever after.

These are called fairy tales.

Yes, it's true, we own that magical box. But whenever I suggested the preposterous notion that we actually turn it on, my husband, Steve's, response was, "DO YOU KNOW HOW EXPENSIVE IT IS TO COOL THIS HOUSE?"

No, I do not.

But neither do you because we've never actually cooled it.

This has been going on for the last thirty years.

We'd be in the middle of a heatwave and our house was the temperature of Mercury. (Or whatever the hottest planet is.) Just trust me, it was toasty.

"Steve, how about we turn on the A/C?" I said, sweat trickling down my face. "I'm dying here."

"You're hot?" Steve asked, genuinely perplexed.

Meanwhile, my internal organs sizzled.

"Do you not see the sweat on my face?" I said, fanning myself.

"Oh, yeah." He nodded and smiled. "You look good. Very glow-y."

I didn't answer.

I just stood there, "glowing."

Steve sighed. "Fine."

A button was clicked and a blast of cold air that until now I had only read about blew through the house.

I stood in front of one of the vents, sucking it all in.

"Sweet holy Freon," I whispered.

A few years later, my friend Chriss and her kids came to visit.

It was the summer of 2008, and once again, the temperatures were in the triple digits. We had just returned from the beach, and upon entering our house, Chriss almost fainted.

"Good God, why is it so hot?" she asked.

Thank you, Chriss. It IS hot.

"Uh, maybe we can turn on the A/C?" she said.

And that's when Steve appeared.

"Yes, we definitely need to turn on the A/C," I said, giving Steve "the look" and nodding towards our guests, who appeared to be melting.

Chriss's kids looked at "Uncle Steve" with their adorable, overheated little faces.

Come on, Steve. Do it for the kids.

"I would," Steve said, "but, unfortunately, it's broken."

I raised an eyebrow.

An appliance that rarely gets used is suddenly broken?

Fishy.

"Don't worry, we'll open some windows and get some nice cross breezes," he said.

This guy was always trying to sell me on "open windows" and "cross breezes."

Think again, Buddy.

Chriss was confused about the whole situation since, according to her, her husband has no problem running the A/C.

She told tales of how the A/C turns on if the house gets above 76 degrees.

"Tell me again how you never get heat stroke in your own house," I said.

It was such a touching story, it brought me to tears.

Nope, that was still sweat.

And you might think it's all about the money, but it's not.

We can be on vacation, and Steve will still manage to regulate the A/C.

"I noticed you REALLY turned down the A/C last night," Steve said, when we were staying at an Italian Airbnb a few years ago.

"Like three degrees," I responded.

"Actually, it was more like five degrees because their units are measured in Celsius," he explained.

I miss the days when he just irritated me in Fahrenheit.

For many years, we continued like this: A hot wife living in a hot house.

(Just to be clear, I mean, "sweaty-hot," not "hot-hot.")

Then about a year ago, everything changed.

It was late August, and the temperature was in the high 90s.

I had just returned from the grocery store, expecting to walk into Casa de La Fuega, and instead, I was greeted by the sweet breeze of artificial air.

"Steve!" I yelled.

Silence…

Except for the A/C running at full blast.

"Steve!" I called again, my concern growing.

Obviously, he had been kidnapped and in the process the kidnappers had turned on the A/C.

I'm gonna miss that guy.

But also, the house felt great.

Steve galloped down the stairs. "Shh," he said. "Holland's napping."

"But the air is on," I said.

"I know," he said. "Poor thing was starting to sweat."

You know who else has been sweating for the last thirty years?!

"She's not going to sleep well if she's hot," he explained.

You don't say.

"Gotta keep my little angel cool," Steve said, smiling.

He turned down the thermostat a few more degrees.

72 DEGREES?!

Who knew thermostats went that low?

We've been running the A/C ever since.

Thank you, Holland!

The only downside is that we can now answer the question, "*do you know how much it costs to cool this house?*"

The answer is...

A lot!

Chapter 5 - Planes, Trains, and Newbers

*Upon completing my first Uber ride, it's not like I expected a trophy.
A sticker would have been nice.*

Newber

It's been around a while, but I've been too nervous to try it. It's easy if you're young or more experienced, but I'm neither of these. Also, there was something about that word that paralyzed me. I just couldn't wrap my mind around those four letters.

Then, this past summer, stranded at an Indianapolis Airport, I had no choice. The time had come to face my fears. So, with a mixture of anxiety and trepidation, I tried something I thought I never would.

Uber.

Quincey, who was supposed to pick me up, had lost her car keys. "I'm sorry," she said on the phone. "You should probably just Uber."

"I guess I could Uber," I said, hoping I was using the word correctly. I'm still not sure if Uber is a noun or a verb, or maybe an adjective?

I'm uber excited to take my first Uber ride!

I didn't even know where to start. Do I just start yelling, "Uber! Uber!" like I was calling for a lost kitten. "Hey, little Uber…"

Obviously, I didn't do that. I'm not a moron.

"Hey, Uber," I whispered into my phone. "Are you in there?" I stared at my phone, hoping my gentle tone would coax an Uber connection.

Twenty minutes later, after googling Uber, and through a series of trial and error, mostly error, I discovered that you neither call out for Uber, nor do you call Uber. Instead, there is an app (and not the yummy kind you eat before dinner) that must be installed.

After another twenty minutes, a forgotten password was retrieved and entered, and *voila*, an Uber App appeared on my phone.

I'm not going to lie to you. I was frightened.

The Uber App is a black square, with a white circle inside. Inside the circle is a smaller black square, with a thin line that cuts the circle horizontally. I have no idea what the Uber muckety-mucks were thinking when they created this logo, but it screams political uprising.

My Nextdoor Neighbor app is a logo of a house. Twitter is a little bird. I wonder If Uber considered any other options, like, I don't know... maybe a CAR!

I clicked on the app. A map appeared. Now that's more like it.

Where to? It asked me.

I put in an address.

Instantly, I was told my driver will be at Ground Transportation in ten minutes (I don't want to brag, but I had already located Ground Transportation and was standing in the designated area)

I studied the app, realizing not only did it tell me my driver's name, but it had her picture in a tiny oval in the bottom right, along with the make of her car and license plate number. But the real kicker was the little car that moved on the app. Linda is eight minutes away. Linda is six minutes away. Linda is three minutes away. Every minute, the car was coming closer. What a rush!

Before I knew it, my app told me Linda has arrived, and *poof!* Just like Cinderella in her carriage, Linda appeared in her Civic.

"Hi, I'm Linda," she said, getting out of the car. I introduced myself as she put my luggage in the trunk.

And that's when the panic hit.

Do I sit in front or back?

If it's a cab ride, obviously I sit in the back. But this is Uber, and Uber is a whole new world.

As a *Newber* (one new to Uber), I cursed myself for not googling Uber etiquette. In the time I had just stood there like a simpleton, mesmerized by the tiny traveling car, I could have figured this out.

Hmm, if I sit in the back, I appear cold and distant.

But, if I sit in the front, I come off as intrusive and creepy.

I opened the front passenger door and slid in, hoping she might mistake intrusive and creepy for enthusiastic.

I smiled at Linda, who returned the smile. Clearly, I had made the right choice.

The drive from the airport to my Airbnb was a 20-minute ride. We talked about travel and family. She told me about her high school kids, and I talked about my college-age kids. It was all very pleasant.

But all I could think was, *I'm doing it, I'm really doing it!*

We weren't there yet. But unless she crashed, which I doubted because she seemed like a competent driver, or she murdered me, which I also doubted, because she didn't have a murdery vibe, I was going to make it.

Linda exited the freeway.

"You know, this is my first-time using Uber," I confessed.

"Really?" she replied. Then she started telling me about which colleges her daughter was interested in.

"I didn't know it would be so easy," I added.

"Oh, yeah, Uber's great," she said, and then went back to naming colleges.

Um, yeah, Uber is great Linda, but you know who else is great? Me! When this day started, I knew nothing of Uber, but look at me now!

It's not like I was expecting a trophy.

A sticker would be nice.

"Here we are," Linda said, pulling up next to a charming barn-style house. We both got out of the car.

"Well, thanks," I said.

"You're welcome."

Is this where I tell her I conquered my Uber fears? Should we hug? High-five?

She reached back into the car and grabbed something.

I *am* going to get a sticker!

She pulled out my glasses case that had fallen out of my purse and handed it to me.

And that was that.

During the trip I took Uber three more times, and it did not disappoint. The thrill one gets when an address is entered, a driver identified, and a tiny car travels closer and closer…

Jerrel is five minutes away.

Luis is two minutes away.

Emily has arrived.

There's nothing like an Uber high!

And on all the rides, I continued to sit in the front, which I later shared with my daughter.

"It's just like a cab ride," my daughter said. "You sit in the back."

"But that seems so impersonal," I said.

My daughter sighed. "You're not on a road trip with a buddy."

But it felt like a road trip with a buddy.

In fact, on my recent Uber ride with Jerrel, we talked about the best waterparks in Indiana. You don't get that kind of road trip-esque banter if you're sitting in the back.

My last Uber ride of the trip occurred when I arrived at LAX. Steve called to tell me he wouldn't be able to pick me up for an hour.

Does nobody in my family want to pick me up?

We were supposed to have breakfast at a coffee shop a few miles from the airport.

"I'll meet you at the restaurant," I told him, exiting the terminal. "I'll Uber there."

"I don't know," he said. "Uber at LAX is tricky."

Apparently, my husband wasn't aware of my Uber capabilities.

Once again, I clicked on what was becoming my favorite app. Yoon would be there in twenty-five minutes. That's a longer wait than I anticipated, but silver lining…that's twenty-five minutes of the tiny traveling car!

As I waited, a businessman, standing next to me, let out a stream of exasperated sighs as he angrily punched keys on his iPhone.

I tore my eyes from the tiny car. "What's the matter?" I asked.

He shook his head. "This app isn't working."

Turns out his app for another car service, which I won't mention, but rhymes with miffed, wasn't loading. *And* he didn't have the Uber app.

What moron doesn't have Uber on his phone?

I checked my phone. "My Uber will be here in fifteen," I told him. "I'm only going a couple miles, so you're welcome to share."

Businessman, who I later learned also went by Mark, looked at me. "Are you allowed to do that?"

Can one request an Uber ride and then brazenly add another rider, who is going to a different destination?

I looked at Yoon's tiny oval face on my phone. He seemed like the kind of driver that would allow it.

"Sure," I said.

When Yoon arrived fifteen minutes later, I explained the situation.

"This isn't how it normally works," Yoon said.

I gave Yoon an *I know this is not the usual Uber procedure, but why don't we help this chump out?*

Yoon popped the trunk and picked up our luggage. "Okay, fine," he told Mark. "Just enter the address you're going to and request me as a driver."

Mark got into the back seat. He stared blankly at his phone. For the first time in my Uber travels, I too got into the back seat.

Sorry Yoon.

As we pulled away from the curb, I helped Mark install the Uber app.

He had a lot to learn.

R-rated Car

A few months back we decided to sell my 2005 Honda Pilot. It was looking pretty shabby, so Steve hired a guy named John to detail it.

Halfway through the detailing, I went outside to give John some water. John turned off his specialized cleaning machine. (No, it wasn't a vacuum. I *know* what a vacuum is.) He was breathing hard, sweating, and appeared to be traumatized. "Your husband didn't warn me," he said, taking a swig of water and catching his breath.

"Sorry," I said.

"Let me guess, your daughter has been driving this car and this is the first time it's ever been detailed."

"Yep," I said, throwing my daughter under the bus or, in this case, the dirty car.

And when I say dirty, it's not *that* bad. If I were to compare it to movies, it's maybe R-rated dirty. Those 17 and older can handle it. Well, except John.

Mostly, it's just make-up all over the interior. Can I help that I'm an excellent multi-tasker and put foundation on as I drive? This results in both my face and the steering wheel having a nice shade of ivory glow.

My husband, who prefers a smudge-free interior, has forbidden me from putting make-up on in his car.

It's like going through airport security in my front driveway.

"Let me see your hands."

Palms out. Inspects hands. Nods.

"Make-up bag."

Removes foundation from bag. Shakes head.

"I'm not going to use it," I say.

Returns foundation to bag. Bag secured in locked trunk.

Apparently, my make-up is not a carry-on.

John returns to cleaning the inside and I admire the exterior. The smudges and dents have been buffed out. It is smooth and clean, as if John shot the car with Botox.

Unfortunately, not even car Botox can take care of the cracked and dangling left bumper. I, I mean my daughter has run into the bushes numerous times. And with each new hit, the bumper cracks a little more and must be shoved into place a little harder.

She should be more careful.

Two hours later, John finally finishes. He's still sweating and has a far-away look in his eyes, like he's seen things he doesn't want to talk about.

He holds up a small trash can. "Ironically, this was the cleanest thing in the car."

I exhale in disgust. "Teenagers."

John puts his hands on his head and looks at the car.

Did he just shudder?

Am I going to have to pay for his therapy?

"It looks amazing," I say.

A smile returns to his face. Thank God, we didn't break him.

"Do not let your daughter drive this car."

"Oh, I won't," I say. "In fact, I will be having a talk with her later."

And I'm not lying.

The talk will be, *Here's $20. If you ever run into John, it was all you.*

AirPain

Blissfully unaware of what Flight #170 had in store for us.

Flight 170 from Burbank to Seattle had trouble written all over it.

"Folks, it appears there is a significant storm developing," the ticket agent announced. "We're going to board immediately, in order to beat the storm.

I sure hope we win.

As promised, Steve and I were quickly herded onto the plane.

The next announcement came from the captain.

This initial introduction is important. The captain's *calm* demeanor is what puts the passengers at ease.

"Uh, yeah…hey, so umm…well…" he trailed off.

I said calm, not stoned.

"So, yeah… there seems to be, um, a situation…"

This was followed by silence.

Were we supposed to guess the situation?

After a long pause, Captain Spicoli continued, "Um, because of the high winds and short runway, uh…we're not able to take off (longer pause)…the plane is a little..."

And that was it.

I don't know what was more concerning, the short runway, the high winds, or the fact that our captain couldn't form complete sentences.

The plane is a little…?

Twenty minutes later we got our answer.

"So, uh…the plane is a little…heavy.

We waited twenty minutes for "heavy?"

"Uh…we're going to dump some fuel, and um…recalculate the numbers," the captain said. "We don't want to kick anybody off because of um…the weight."

Was he serious?

Was there a scale on board?

Why did I wear so many layers?

On the upside, he knew the definition of "recalculate" and used it correctly in the sentence.

Ten minutes later, our captain announced some semi-good news.

"Uh, yeah…I think we're going to try and, um, take off."

TRY?

Let's lose the try. Just take off.

My telepathic motivational speech must have reached him because after some white knuckles, our super-sized plane managed to depart from our under-sized runway.

A little shaky at first, but then the winds calmed, the plane stopped swaying, and like an angel from heaven, something beautiful appeared:

BEVERAGE SERVICE!

Flight Attendant Debby started in the front of the plane, and as passengers of row 29, we had a long wait. However, good things come to those who wait, and soon we were only eight rows away…six rows…three rows…

Then, bump, rattle, whoosh! The plane rocked sideways, and before I could say, *Pinot please*, Flight Attendant Debby and her aluminum box of fun disappeared…

and the captain reappeared.

"So, um, yeah, folks…we're hitting some turbulence."

Thank you, Captain Obvious.

It was as if we were in a giant washing machine.

Windows rattled, tray tables thudded, lights flickered.

"This is bad," Steve commented.

Thank you, Passenger Obvious.

I peered at the oxygen mask. I know it's there in case of emergency, and oxygen is a pretty nifty idea, but you know what would be even better?

Sippy cups of emergency wine that deploy from the ceiling.

It doesn't have to be fancy, just a house red that drops into your lap.

Did I just invent something?

After half an hour of being tossed around mercilessly, the winds subsided, and the plane leveled.

The lights came on, and the intercom crackled.

I braced myself for words of wisdom from Captain Spicoli, but this was a female voice, and she spoke in hushed tones.

"Elaine? Elaine?" she called. A few deep breaths before one final, "Elaine?"

Then click.

Silence.

Was Elaine another flight attendant?

A passenger?

Were they summoning her from the great beyond?

The hairs on my arm stood up. It was like I was part of a supernatural airplane horror film.

Did I just invent a new genre?

Half an hour later, the flight took a turn for the better (aeronautical pun intended). Debby and her magical elixirs finally made it to the good people of row 29. "What will you have?" she asked.

Hmm, what pairs well with imminent death?

"Cab," I answered.

"Same," Steve said.

She wiped the sweat from her forehead. "I tell you, I'm not even a drinker, but after a night like this…"

That's not a phrase you want to hear from your flight attendant.

After filling our cups, my husband held his up.

"Here's to…" he started.

"A quick and painless death," I finished.

Cheers!

For the rest of the flight, the turbulence lessened, and we enjoyed our wine and dinner. And when I say dinner, I'm referring to my sad sack of pretzels.

As Debby refilled my water, I whispered, "Who's Elaine?"

"Tray tables up," she answered.

"Did you hear that?" I said to my husband.

"Yes, tray tables up."

"Not that. She ignored me when I asked about Elaine."

"Is it possible we heard it wrong?" he asked. "Maybe instead of *Elaine, Elaine*, they were saying, *the plane, the plane*."

I digested this new information, nodding. "Like Tattoo, on Fantasy Island."

This flight had a lot of layers to it.

Twenty minutes later, our captain threw out some sentence fragments and we began nosediving.

I guess that meant we were landing.

However, this landing felt more like one of those carnival rides, where you're freefalling from ridiculous heights, screaming in terror, and thinking, *why did I put my life in the hands of a carny*?

As we plummeted to our demise, all I could think was, *I wish that carny was our pilot.*

To say we came in hot was an understatement.

There were screeches, sparks and burning rubber. We may have lost a wheel.

The plane tilted to one side as we skidded along the runway.

I held my breath.

The skidding eventually slowed to a gentle lurching, then one final screech, and…

We stopped.

Along with the other passengers, we couldn't get off that plane fast enough.

Outside the cockpit, Flight Attendant Debs popped a Xanax and bid us good night.

Looking past Debs, I attempted to catch a glimpse of our pilot. I needed to know, who was this menace to the sky? And then I saw something: huddled in the corner of the cockpit was a small figure.

Was that a toddler?

Was this "Take Your Child to Work" day?

If so, well done, kid.

As I exited Flight 170, I pondered other questions:

Would "Elainegate" ever be solved?

Who can help me market SCEW (Sippy Cups of Emergency Wine)?

And most importantly:

Were our return trip tickets refundable?

Acai Ya Later

I was getting ready to take the train home from my friend, Chriss's house, when suddenly, I had a hankering for an acai bowl.

I began pulling out ingredients: strawberries, blueberries, almond milk, bananas.

It was all going so well, until…

"Chriss, where's your peanut butter?" I asked, scouring her cupboards.

Chriss peered over my shoulder. "Hmm," she said. "I guess we're out."

OUT OF PEANUT BUTTER?!

Was she a lunatic?

Possibly.

Fortunately, there was a smoothie place a mile from her house and my train didn't leave until 1:49.

I walked into *Juice it Up!* at 1:06.

(Sidenote: I admire shops that have an exclamation point in their name. It feels like they care a little more.)

"I'll have two acai berry bowls," I told the elderly man who took my order.

I gave Chriss, who was waiting in the car outside, a thumbs up.

The man handed my order to a younger woman, who began pouring concoctions into the blender.

She had three blenders going at once.

This woman knew how to JUICE! IT! UP!

Meanwhile, the man just stood there.

He smiled.

I smiled back.

I didn't want to tell him how to do his job, but maybe he could do a little chopping while his co-worker was blending?

I checked my watch.

1:12.

The blender whirled.

The man smiled. "How are you today?"

"I'm good," I said.

More whirling, more smiling.

Sadly, no chopping.

Finally, the woman poured the smoothie mixture into two bowls and set it on the counter.

1:19.

I was starting to sweat.

The man stared at the bowls.

Then he studied the photo of the Acai Berry Bowl, hanging from the wall.

He eyed the containers of fruit.

He glanced back at the picture.

IT'S STRAWBERRIES AND BANANAS! STOP LOOKING AT YOUR FRUIT CLIFF NOTES AND START CHOPPING!

I took a breath, trying to remain calm.

I didn't complain.

After all, I had once been a waitress.

Quite possibly, World's Worst Waitress.

I worked at Marie Calendars in the late '80s and if I ever waited on you, let me just say, *I'm sorry, and your pot pie should be out shortly.*

The man *sliced* strawberries.

Slicing implies a quick movement.

The man sculpted strawberries.

1:26.

Once the strawberries were chiseled to perfection, he strategically placed them in the bowl.

Then he studied the picture on the wall again.

BANANAS COMES NEXT! THERE'S ONLY TWO INGREDIENTS! HOW DID YOU PASS YOUR JUICE IT UP *EXAM?!*

If I thought I was going to die a slow, painful death over the strawberries, the banana preparation took it to a whole new level.

The manner in which he peeled the banana could only be described as...

Tenderly.

Which is all fine and good, except…

FOR THE LOVE OF GOD, STOP UNDRESSING MY BANANA! (Sorry, that sounded pervy) *JUST RIP IT OFF! NEVER MIND, I'LL EAT THE PEEL!*

1:33.

When he adorned the acai bowls with the last banana slice, he picked up a dispenser of agave or arsenic (at this point, who cares) and drizzled it over the top.

"I'll be right back," he said, disappearing into the back room.

NOOOOOOOOOO!

He returned with a cardboard container.

1:35.

Very slowly and precisely, he secured the bowls into the containers, as if they were life-saving organs, about to be transported.

He smiled and held up his masterpiece, which I grabbed.

"They look delicious!" I yelled, running out the door and jumping into Chriss's car.

1:39.

The train station was ten minutes away.

Chriss accelerated down main roads, swerving around corners, barely avoiding near death collisions.

We may have been airborne at one point.

She was *The Fast and The Furious*, *Dukes of Hazzard*, and *Herbie Fully Loaded*, all rolled into one.

"Don't worry," she yelled as she sped past a semi. "The train will probably be late."

No, Chriss, the train is only late if you're early.

We screeched into the parking lot at 1:47.

I grabbed my backpack, purse, and acai bowl. Chriss pulled out my suitcase.

The train was already there.

On the far track.

That meant, we had to sprint up three flights of stairs, run over a bridge, and then race down another set of stairs.

It's fun to run in flip-flops!

"Irvine train passengers, last call!" the conductor announced over the loudspeaker.

"WAIT, WAIT, WAIT!" I holler-begged, as I ran toward the train employee who was standing on the platform and yelling, "DOORS ARE CLOSING!"

The Train Man shook his head at me in utter disappointment. "Hurry up," he said, ushering me onto the train.

"Just a minute," I said, looking around frantically. "My friend has my suitcase."

He shook his head again.

Chriss, he's not happy with you either.

"Where is she?" he asked.

"She's coming, I swear, she's just not as fast as me," I said, and then added. "She's disabled."

That's when Chriss came barreling down the stairs, my suitcase in one hand, high over her head, as if charging into battle.

The Train Man rolled his eyes and sighed because I was late *and* a liar.

But the good news was Chriss passed off my suitcase like a champ and I made my train.

More importantly, I got to enjoy "World's Most Beautiful Acai Bowl."

I just wish they hadn't forgotten the peanut butter.

Now Boarding (everyone, but you)

Whenever I book a flight, I always end up in Group 7.

Even when I check in twenty-four hours ahead of time, ON THE DOT!

Tappity-tappity-tap-tap-tap! (That's me typing like a madman, hoping to beat my fellow passengers, and secure a decent boarding number.) But when my boarding pass pops up...

GROUP 7!

(Am I competing against professional typists?)

Group 7 is the equivalent of being picked last in PE.

Except the ticket agents are the captains, and not only do they not want me on their team, but they also don't think I deserve any overhead bin space.

But I'm not always in Group 7. Sometimes, I'm Group E.

"E" as in EVERYONE gets to board, but you!

This is why I decided it was time to try a new airline…

Delta.

When my boarding pass popped up, I almost fell out of my chair.

Main Cabin #2!

Are you kidding me?!

It was like I was a silver medalist.

Delta likes me! They really like me!

I stood at my gate, beaming, boarding pass in hand, facing upward, in perfect scanning position.

"In just a few minutes, we will begin boarding," the agent announced in a cheery voice.

I extended my arm back and positioned my carry-on, so it was ready to roll. My right leg was forward, knee slightly bent. Obviously, I had already stretched.

"We will start with our Delta One passengers," the agent gushed, blowing them kisses.

That must be their fancy name for First Class.

That's okay, Main Cabin One will be next, and then, Moi!

After all the fancy pants people boarded, the agent announced, "Active Military, you may now board." She saluted them.

Not going to argue that one. Also, thank you for your service.

I edged forward. At any moment she'll be calling the good folks of Main Cabin #2.

"First Class and Delta Premium, you may now board." The agent gave them a round of applause.

I thought Delta One was First Class. And what's this Delta Premium you speak of?

More fancy, smug people boarded.

But I didn't lose faith. I was so close.

"We now invite our Diamond Medallion members to board," the agent beamed.

I sighed.

As if I could compete with a club based on diamonds and medallions.

However, most of the Diamond Medallion members wore neither diamonds nor medallions, so obviously it was a club based on lies.

"Families with small children, you may now board," the agent said, giving a thumbs up to the frazzled parents and their screaming toddler, who kept neither his hands nor his bronchial cough to himself.

But I had bigger problems. The herd had thinned, and overhead bin space was diminishing. I knew I had to get the ball rolling.

I raised my fist in the air. "Main Cabin! Main Cabin! Main Cabin!" I chanted, trying to engage my fellow main cabin passengers. But they were a listless bunch, completely devoid of team spirit.

I slumped against a pillar as the agent welcomed, "Delta Comfort."

Still smiling, but with her enthusiasm waning, she announced, "Sky Priority, you may board."

A bunch of average Joes shuffled past me.

I'm losing to these guys?

"We will now board Main Cabin #1," she said, forcing a smile.

The below-average Joes boarded.

When there was only us riffraff left, the agent yawned, "Main Cabin #2...I guess."

I dragged myself over to the agent. After scanning my boarding pass, she said, "We're out of overhead bin space, so you'll need to--"

"Yeah, yeah, yeah," I sighed, handing her my carry-on.

That's what happens when you're in Main Cabin #2.

Which is the equivalent of Group 9.

Also known as Group I.

And we all know what "I" stands for...

I can't believe I was excited about Main Cabin #2!

Chapter 6 - Nina and Alvin

They gave me life. The least I could do is give them a chapter.

Let me introduce you to my parents, Nina and Alvin. Nina, who is 78 and Alvin, who is 88 have been married for 58 years. Nina and Alvin are not their real names; when I told them I was going to write a few stories about them, they requested aliases.

"Please call us Nina and Alvin."

Nina and Alvin, it is.

Nina and Alvin, on Movies

Nina and Alvin have certain criteria when it comes to seeing movies. They will only see movies that start no earlier than 3:45 and no later than 5:15. If you don't believe me, check their ticket stubs. There is a strict 90-minute window in which they begin their cinematic experience.

You can invite them to see *A Star Is Born* at 3:30 at Regal Cinema 16, but Nina will then inform you that it's playing at 4:15 at Jann's Marketplace.

Enjoy your 4:15 showing.

Equally important as the movie's time is the location of the seats in the theater. If you think you can just willy-nilly pick a seat anywhere, you are sadly mistaken. Nina and Alvin only sit in the last row, in the second and third seats from the aisle. Except for the first twenty minutes of the film, in which Alvin will be sitting directly in front of Nina.

Why would Alvin do this?

That's what I wanted to know.

It was a few years back and I had met my parents for a 4:30 showing of *A Man Called Ove*. Walking into the theater, I spotted my mom, who was already sitting in her self-assigned seat. I took the seat next to her. "Where's Dad?" I asked.

"Hi honey," my dad said, turning around. He was sitting in the chair directly in front of my mom.

The lights dimmed, he returned his gaze to the screen and the previews began.

Hmm, this is interesting.

After about the fifth preview, when I realized that I was not going to get an explanation, I whispered to my mom, "Why isn't Dad sitting with us?"

"Oh, he will, but for right now, we are just making sure nobody sits in front of us," she said. "We don't want anybody blocking our view."

I scanned the theater. Besides us, there was just one elderly couple in the second row. Their tiny silver heads were barely visible.

"You mean like those thugs?" I asked.

"Exactly," Nina answered.

Another thing that Nina and Alvin have strict guidelines about is popcorn. If you accompany them to the movie and casually remark, "Hey, maybe we should get some popcorn…"

Nina will respond, "No, no, no, no, no, no." If Nina is emphatic about something there will be multiple "nos."

No explanation.

Just "No," and then five more "nos."

It doesn't matter if you offer to pay, the answer will always be "No."

And it's not like they don't like popcorn. They have a big bag of popcorn in their pantry right now. I'm not lying, you can check.

But I guess it's the movie popcorn they're violently opposed to. They literally won't eat one delicious buttery kernel.

"Do you want some?" I offered the bag to my mom.

"No, no, no, no, no, no," she said.

"Dad?" I asked.

He turned around, "No thank you."

Do they both suffer from some deep seeded childhood movie popcorn trauma?

With Nina and Alvin, you never know.

You'd think with how particular Nina and Alvin are about seat selection and movie popcorn repression, they would be equally picky when choosing their movies.

You would be wrong.

A couple of years back, they decided to see the movie *Sausage Party*.

"You do realize it's not a documentary on Jimmy Dean?" I asked.

"Oh, we know," Nina said.

"And you are aware that the target audience for this movie is 17-year-old boys?" I added.

"Excellent," Alvin replied.

So they went, they saw, they critiqued.

"It was a bit disturbing," Nina admitted.

"We didn't realize the sausages would be animated," Alvin said.

As opposed to real-life human sausages?

Regardless, Nina and Alvin continue to see every movie ever made. Last week they saw *The Lego Movie,* yesterday they watched *Roma,* and next week, one can only guess.

Perhaps *Sausage Party 2.*

Nina the Pusher

Nina may seem like the grandmother next door, but there is another side to her. Nina is a hard-core, in your face, straight-up pusher.

Oxycodone? Heroine? Opioids?

Bigger.

Grisham. King. Clancy.

It started about thirty years ago. Back then, it was the small stuff, mostly newspaper articles. A heartwarming Erma Bombeck story. A cautionary tale on the dangers of sun exposure (Should have read that one thoroughly.) A feature on the ten most profitable college majors (like creative writing?).

Over the years, the articles kept coming. Then, about fifteen years ago, when Nina retired, she upped her game. It was no longer, "Psst, want to try some weed?"

It was a big bag of meth delivered to my front porch.

Nina had become a die-hard book pusher. Now that she had more time on her hands, she was reading like a fiend and eager to distribute.

"Hi, Mom, how's your day?"

"Better than Anna's," she said, shaking her head. "No one believes her about the murder."

"Who did Anna murder?"

"Nobody, she witnessed a murder." Nina sighed. "*Woman in the Window*, you should read it."

"I'm kind of busy..."

The following day it appeared on my kitchen counter.

Nina called an hour later. "Have you started it?"

"Not yet, I still need to finish *Darkest Fear*."

"Remember, *Darkest Fear* is due by Thursday."

Nina wasn't just a book pusher; she was a library book pusher. This meant that not only did I have to finish the book, but I had to do so in a timely manner, otherwise I could kiss 25 cents a day goodbye.

I wasn't the only one Nina was dealing to: My husband, my daughters, and my friends were all regular customers. Nina was no small-time peddler.

On Wednesdays, Nina cruised Ventura County in her minivan, collecting the goods.

At the Thousand Oaks library, she headed straight for the circulation desk, where the requested book was on hold. The exchange was quick; one laminated library card for 438 pages of compelling family drama.

She slipped the stash into her reusable canvas tote. Nina hit one more library and then she was en route to both drop off and pick up.

When she texted that she was twenty minutes away, I had 62 pages left in *Darkest Fear*.

I still didn't know: *Was Jeremy Myron's son? Would the FBI find the kidnappers in time? Would Myron and Emily reconcile?*

I tried to read faster, but my left eye was twitching and the words were blurring.

Sure, I could pretend I finished it, but Nina would be asking questions and vague answers wouldn't cut it. I once told Nina that I had finished a book I hadn't even started. Without saying a word, she returned to the library and renewed the book.

I found it later, in my bed.

As I frantically skimmed the pages of *Darkest Fear*, I could feel Nina getting closer.

Then, with 37 pages to go…

A van door shut. The musty scent of paper and ink wafted through the front window. The light tapping of sensible shoes approached.

I closed the book.

I took a deep breath.

Knock, knock, knock…

On the Road with Nina and Alvin

Nina and Alvin can often be seen zipping around in their 2018 Honda Odyssey.

Nina is always in the driver's seat, hands at 10 and 2, with eyes glued to the road.

But where's Alvin?

Look closely through the tinted windows in the middle row…

There he is!

It's like a modern day "Driving Miss Daisy," but with a man and a minivan.

Alvin is quite comfy, reclining in the back, his feet resting on the center console.

Alvin gets to put his sneakers on the console?

What sort of three-ring circus is Nina running?

Slow down, cowboy, there are rules.

Alvin may put his feet up, if and only if the console is covered with a pre-approved pillow.

Wait a second...Is that Alvin eating in the van?

Yes, Alvin is enjoying apple slices as Nina whisks him off to the Costco Pharmacy.

However, what Alvin may *not* enjoy while being driven to his local hotspots, is a Kerns Guava Smoothie, which he once tried to smuggle into the vehicle.

Leave your roadies at home, Buddy.

Since then, Nina has enforced a clear set of road rules and Alvin appeared to be following them until...

A recent trip to Solvang.

While exiting the freeway, a car cut Nina off. She slammed on the brakes and Alvin went flying!

Luckily, the headrest cushioned the blow and Alvin was fine.

You know who was not fine?

Nina!

She pulled into a Chevron parking lot, shut off the ignition, and turned around.

"Where's your seatbelt?" Nina asked.

Alvin pointed to the metal buckle, lying beside him.

"Why aren't you wearing it?" she demanded.

"It's uncomfortable," Alvin said.

"It's the law," Nina said.

Alvin shrugged.

Alvin thought, at his age, he'd reached his seatbelt quota, and enough was enough.

"Well, we're not going anywhere until you put it on!"

Alvin reminded Nina about the time, when he was in his 20s, and how *not* wearing a seatbelt had saved his life. After a serious crash, he had been thrown from the car, relatively unharmed, while his car had been totaled.

Nina folded her arms.

The afternoon sky turned dusk.

Alvin took a nap…

Unbuckled.

Thirty minutes later, Alvin woke up.

They were still at the Chevron and Nina was working on her crossword, trying to figure out a five-letter word for reckless.

"I'm hungry," Alvin said, opening the car door. "I'm gonna get a Snickers."

Nina shook her head. *Not buckling up? Candy in the car? Snacks before dinner?*

Alvin was turning into a real rebel.

Ten minutes later, they were finally back on the road.

Nina looked in the rearview mirror, pleased to see that Alvin was wearing his seatbelt.

What she was not pleased about was that Alvin had purchased a King Size Snickers *and* a Guava Smoothie.

Oh, the nougat!

Oh, the nectar!

Oh, Alvin!

Vacation Rules

Over the years, we have traveled a lot with Nina and Alvin. Vacationing with these two Super Seniors is a hoot, but if you think this is some loosey goosey vacation, think again!

There are rules, people.

Rule #1 – B.Y.O.P.

When we vacation, Nina always brings delicious treats like wasabi almonds or homemade blueberry muffins. She'll even whip up a batch of her famous tortellini stew.

That Nina loves to share her food.

Well, *most* of her food.

"What's this?" I asked, pointing to a baggie on the second shelf of the refrigerator.

"That's not for you," Nina responded.

"But what is it?" I peered in for a better look.

Nina shut the refrigerator door.

"Those are our prunes," she said. "I packed just enough so your dad and I get two a day."

"That's nice," I said.

"We don't have any extra prunes," she added.

"I don't want…"

"If you wanted prunes, you should have brought your own," Nina said.

Does anyone ever really want prunes?

Steve called out from the other room. "Honey, can you get me something to eat?"

"Sure," I said, opening the refrigerator door. "What do you want?"

Nina took a few steps forward, and like a Mama Bear, she stood between me and her prunes.

I grabbed a plum (prune's far more delicious cousin) and tossed it to Steve.

Nina shut the door once again. "I can't be supplying prunes for everyone."

Did you hear that, folks?

B.Y.O.P! (Bring Your Own Prunes!)

Parker wandered into the kitchen and opened the refrigerator.

She grabbed the bag of prunes. "What's this?"

Nina's head exploded.

Rule #2 – Respect "The Cocktail Hour"

On vacation, we always enjoy Happy Hour with Nina and Alvin.

Except Happy Hour shall be referred to as Cocktail Hour.

Happy Hour is when you're drinking Coronas on a beach, like Snoop Dogg.

Do Nina and Alvin look like Snoop Dogg?

Also, Happy Hour can be anytime. (It's 5:00 somewhere.)

Sophisticated people, such as Nina and Alvin, *never* partake in libations before 8:00.

(Except for that one time in 2014. Nina went for a sunset walk, and Alvin cracked a cold one at 7:45.)

Please don't tell Nina.

As a sophisticated couple of a certain age, you might assume that Nina and Alvin would enjoy sophisticated cocktails such as Martinis or Manhattans.

No, siree.

Nina and Alvin drink Coors Light.

I, too, used to enjoy Coors Light.

In college.

It was low-cal, cheap, and easy to shotgun.

(I'm in no way implying that Nina and Alvin shotgun their beer. I'm also not putting it past them.)

"Are you sure you don't want to try this?" I asked, offering them some of my Hefeweizen.

Alvin shook his head.

Nina scrunched her nose.

We're not interested in your hoppy, zippy, citrusy IPA, with hints of grapefruit.

They both took a sip of their Coors Light.

For Nina and Alvin, it's the Silver Bullet or nothing.

At 8:01, of course.

Rule #3- It's a One-Night Stand: Deal with It

Nina and Alvin have always enjoyed vacationing with us (I think), but they will only agree to spend one night.

Do Nina and Alvin have commitment issues?

On Saturday night, Nina and Alvin informed us that they had things to do the next day.

"What things?" I asked.

"We have things," Nina said, handing Alvin his allotted prunes.

Alvin chewed and nodded. "We're very busy."

Nina and Alvin slept over Saturday night, and we assumed we'd see them in the morning because they said, "See you in the morning."

We, however, did *not* see them in the morning.

The only one who saw them was Parker, who had gotten up to go to the bathroom.

At first, she wasn't sure it was them.

Just two figures, tip-toeing stealth-like, down the hallway around 5 a.m.

Parker rubbed her eyes, still blurry with sleep, "Grandma? Grandpa?" she said.

"We gotta go," Nina whispered, unlocking the latch on the door.

"Where are you going?" Parker asked.

"Shhh, go back to sleep," Alvin said, patting her head.

Then, like the Grinch, he sent Parker Lou Who, who was no more than 22, back to bed.

With suitcases in one hand and prunes in the other, the two of them slipped through the door, into the darkness…

thus, concluding another wild vacation with Nina and Alvin.

The Dynasty

Over the years there have been many dynasties: The Yankees, the Celtics, the Bulls.

But here we are in 2020, living through a pandemic. Football has been canceled and baseball is but a smattering of games, cheered on by cardboard cutouts.

Where are our athletic heroes? Our memorable moments? Will we ever witness the next great dynasty?

Fear not, my sad little spectators, there is a sports dynasty brewing in our midst.

Although this team consists of only two players, Nina and Alvin are a force to be reckoned with.

We discovered this after they invited us for a friendly game of bocce.

We arrived at the courts to find Nina and Alvin, wooden balls in hand, ready for battle.

Alvin's "GAME ON" t-shirt screamed psychological warfare.

Nina's nautical blouse and matching capris were menacing.

But seriously, Nina and Alvin had a collective age of 158 so we were quite sure we could take them.

They beat us 10 - 1.

"Better luck next time, kiddos," Alvin said after the game. This was followed by a simultaneous jump in the air and clicking of the heels.

We played them countless more times, and each time, they destroyed us.

Last week, we had finally had enough. I called an emergency bocce meeting.

"I think the problem is you need to play better," I told Steve.

"Also, you need to play better," Steve countered.

Both solid points.

We also agreed we were not going to let Alvin psych us out with his intimidating t-shirts.

"Ready to play, kiddos?" Alvin asked when he arrived at the courts, wearing his "No Soup for You!" t-shirt.

"I can have soup if I want," I muttered, picking up the ball.

Twenty minutes in, we were down 9-5, but we had just rolled four perfectly placed shots, all within inches of the little white ball.

I could taste victory.

But hold on, folks...

Alvin just called a time out to switch from daytime to nighttime bifocals.

"Much better," he said, adjusting his glasses, and showboating his clear vision.

He handed Nina their last ball and the two huddled.

(Huddling is not normally part of bocce, but I believe these two were using it as an intimidation tactic.)

I'm not scared.

Nina and Alvin chest bumped.

Maybe a little.

Nina stepped on to the sand, eyed her target, and with a flick of her wrist, released her ball.

"Left, left, go left," she yelled.

Her ball veered left, whizzing past her intended target.

"Oh, Nina, too hard! Stupid, stupid, stupid!"

Sometimes Nina gets mad at Nina.

But you can't be a bocce legend, without a little fire. Am I right?

Nina's ball knocked our two balls out of the way.

"Slow, slow, slow…there you go," Nina said.

The ball slowed as Nina had commanded and came to rest, inches from the white ball.

Game Over.

Alvin and Nina high-fived.

"Better luck next time, kiddos!" Alvin said.

Then a wave, a leap, a click of the heels, and they were off.

Steve sighed. "Maybe we shouldn't worry about the score and just enjoy playing with them."

"Or…" I said, "we can find somebody else who can beat them."

Later that night, I invited our kids to the emergency bocce meeting. "Okay, who wants to take down Grandma and Grandpa?"

At first, it was rolling eyes, and "I don't want to beat old people."

Come on, where's your competitive spirit?

Finally, they relented.

"How did it go?" I asked Quincey when she returned from the game.

"Not well," she said. "Also, Grandpa can jump really high."

Colby asked, "How are they so unbeatable?"

I shrugged.

It's truly one of life's great mysteries.

But if you want to see for yourself, check out the Moorpark bocce courts on Tuesday evenings.

There you'll find Nina and Alvin, clad in intimidating apparel, peering through their bifocals, as they roll their way to victory and celebrate with their signature phrase, "Better luck next time, kiddos!"

Just like any great dynasty.

Game on, Nina and Alvin!

Chapter 7- Oh, the Horror!

At night, from a distance, I still look pretty good. If you're inebriated, even better.

Gobble, Gobble

I won a writing contest last week. It was a 100-word short story for the local paper. The editor, who called to tell me I'd won, interviewed me over the phone, and just as we were finishing, he added, "And we'll need a picture."

"Of me?" I asked.

"Yes."

"How about someone related to me?"

"Nope."

"Or a middle-aged actress that resembles me?"

The editor was probably wishing he had selected a sane person.

"Fine," I said.

There must be one decent picture of me.

I began frantically searching through my phone and computer. I emailed my daughter. *If there's a good picture of me, please send!*

And she did.

Oh, the horror! Who is this less attractive, older version of myself?

Finally, I found a picture that was flattering. It was far away, blurry, and the person next to me partially obstructed my face.

Jackpot!

The editor was less impressed. "We need a clear solo unfiltered photo."

A **clear** picture? Since when is clear better? For a glass of water, perhaps. But for pictures, let's not discount hazy. Sometimes I see a picture of myself without my glasses and I think, "Hey, I look good." Then I put my glasses on to confirm and I cry a little inside.

A **solo** picture? Who has a solo picture of themselves, besides realtors and convicts?

An unfiltered picture of myself? Filters were invented for a reason. And I don't mind sending an unfiltered picture of myself, as long as *you*, the editor, do the filtering on your end. And I'd like that in writing.

After not finding a single, clear, solo, unfiltered picture of myself, I realized I would have to take a selfie. I examined my middle-aged face. Not bad. But really my face wasn't the problem.

It was my neck.

I didn't even know necks could be a problem until one of my friends (who will remain nameless, but we'll call her Carrie) recently told me about her neck woes. "I hate my neck," she said. "It's gotten so saggy, like a turkey. *Well, that doesn't sound fun*, I thought, glancing in the mirror at my own neck. Oh, my God! When did this happen? The lines, the wrinkles, the loose skin. Maybe it wasn't full-blown turkey, but it was turkey-esque.

I checked my watch. Did I have time for some light surgery?

Probably not.

But I did have tape.

My friend once told me how she used tape to lift her eyebrows and soften the lines in between. That Carrie sure is resourceful.

But tape on a neck? Wasn't this going too far?

I decided 3M duct tape would work best.

We were out of clear tape, so I used red. I cut a piece, and while holding the tape in one hand, I pushed the left side of my neck back with the other hand. Carefully, I tucked the loose skin under the tape on the back of my neck. This stuff is amazing, I thought as I secured the rest of my turkey neck into place. The skin was firm, taught, years younger. Perfect.

Uh, oh.

I could see red on one side. Not a lot, but enough that might make one ponder the question, "Is this a vampire story?"

The second time, I cut a *small* piece of tape and neatly pulled the left side of my neck into place. *Looking good, left side.* But as I attempted to attach the right side, I ran out of tape. One side was smooth. The other, saggy. I was a before and after advertisement for turkey neck.

I found more tape and on my third attempt, I finally got it. The skin was pulled back evenly on both sides without a hint of vampire or sag.

Just right.

I felt like Goldilocks, if Goldilocks were a deranged writer with neck issues. Maybe she was. We know so little about her.

After make-up and hair, I went in search of the best possible lighting in the house. It required me to spin around in several rooms, until I found optimum lighting. Slightly dizzy, but satisfied that I had done all I could, I snapped six selfies. Within minutes, I had made my selection, and one picture of a middle-aged neurotic writer, with a good neck, was en route to the editor.

His response was, "Thanks."

Thanks?

144

How about,

You're so brave…

I know these last 24 hours have been trying…

We were wrong to make you go through this…

The following week, my story, a short article on me, and the picture came out. My family, friends and colleagues had many kind words.

"What a great story."

"I love the ending."

"The imagery was powerful."

I thanked them politely, feeling a sense of pride. Still, it would have been nice if just one person had commented, "You know what was even smoother than your transitions, your neck."

Flotation Device

On our first day in Hawaii, Steve and I went to the dive shop to rent snorkel gear.

While the salesgirl, Molly, was ringing us up, Steve said, "I'm so excited for our surf lesson."

"I can't wait to kayak," I said.

"Hopefully we'll have time to paddleboard," Steve added.

Molly smiled, obviously impressed with our athletic prowess.

Surfing! Kayaking! Paddle boarding!

What a spry, young couple!

Molly handed us our snorkel and fins. "Anything else?" she asked.

"I think we're good," Steve said.

"Are you sure?" she asked. "Maybe a flotation device?"

DID SHE JUST SAY FLOTATION DEVICE?!

Does she think we're two years old?

Or 102?

"We're good," Steve said.

"The swells have been pretty big lately," Molly said. "Last week I had to save six Canadians."

Molly then went into a dramatic reenactment of how she single-handedly rescued six Canadians from near death.

I think perhaps Molly tells tall tales.

But I wasn't really listening to how Molly saved half a dozen hosers.

All I heard was *flotation device.*

Well, we showed her.

We went surfing and our instructor said we were naturals.

He said it with his eyes.

Our kayaking and paddle board skills were nothing short of masterful.

Masterful, mediocre, whatever.

After each activity, Steve and I would shake our heads and scoff, "Flotation device!"

On the second to last day, we went snorkeling.

The usual calm waters were choppy, threatening to push us into the rocks.

I guess Molly wasn't a total liar.

But a flotation device?

Nice try, Molly.

As the water became increasingly rough, Steve and I decided to head in.

We were about 50 yards from shore when a ginormous wave appeared.

"WATCH OUT!" Steve warned before being pounded by the wave.

I turned just in time to have the same wall of water crash down upon me.

Because I was still wearing my mask, I was able to clearly see the wave pummeling me.

Water, sand, water, sand, water, sand.

Good news: I can still do a somersault!

The ocean finally spit us both out on shore.

We tried to help each other up (with fins still on) and ended up toppling over, entangled in one another.

Picture *From Here to Eternity,* but with less sex appeal and more snorkel gear.

The good news is we did *not* need a flotation device.

Which is what we reminded ourselves of at the airport the following day.

"Flotation device," Steve scoffed, as we made our way through security.

"Especially with how we rode those waves," I said, walking through the X-ray machine.

Rode waves, pummeled by waves, same thing.

And that's when the beeping went off.

I removed clothing.

Beep, beep, beep.

I removed jewelry.

Beep, beep, beep.

"I don't know what it could be," I said.

The TSA agent sized me up.

"A hip replacement will set off the alarm," he said.

I miss the days when people just thought I needed a flotation device.

Miracle

When I first walked into the building, ominous music played as if I were entering a horror film.

Like Clarice, I could hear the lambs screaming.

BAAAAHH!

Wait, no, that was me.

"Can I help you?" Brittany, the salesclerk asked.

It would help if I were thirty years younger and ten pounds lighter, but Brittany didn't appear to be a wizard.

"I'm fine," I said, searching through a sea of suits.

Next to the aquatic swim skirts was a row of skimpy bikinis.

"Is this the women's or the juniors?" I asked.

"Both," Brittany beamed. "We've combined them for more choices."

Normally, I'm all for integration, but *not* when it comes to swimsuits. Bathing suit shopping is torturous enough without visual reminders of what you will never wear again.

Segregate the suits, Brittany.

Twenty minutes later, I headed to the dressing room.

How many did I try on?

20? 30? 1,000?

It's a numbers game.

A few were horrific, like the one that had horizontal straps all the way up the sides.

Newsflash: I do not look good in venetian blinds.

The pile of nylon carnage grew.

Just as I was about to give up hope, something encouraging happened… the blue suit, with ruffles in all the right places was…

I don't want to brag, but…

Not offensive.

Unfortunately, I made the mistake of leaving the security of the dimly lit dressing room to check it out in the full-length hallway mirror.

BRIGHT LIGHTS!

BACK FAT!

BAAAAHH!

I raced back inside the safety of my dressing room.

It's okay, I reassured myself, *it's not like I'm going to be seen under bright lights in real life.*

But then, I recalled the sun.

As I took my Walk of Shame back to the bathing suit department to select some more sad suits, Brittany popped up behind a counter.

She was a stealthy little salesclerk.

"Can I get you anything?" Brittany asked.

I doubted Brittany had my youth behind that counter, so I shook my head.

I dragged my feet, meandering through the endless forest of bathing suits and then…

Suddenly...

The heavens opened, the angels sang, and a rack of bathing suits with a sign advertising that I would look "ten pounds lighter in ten minutes" appeared.

I had discovered the holy grail of bathing suits.

THE MIRACLE SUIT!

The tag on the suit showed a smiling woman, pleased with her Miracle Suit purchase. And although I didn't know this woman, she appeared honest and, more importantly, ten pounds lighter.

I selected an array of these magical suits and practically skipped back to the dressing room.

I tried on a purple flowery number, and...

Abra-frickin'-cadabra!

Lumps, bumps and ten pounds had vanished!

I twirled, trying to see where it all was hiding.

My elbows? My toes? My earlobes?

Who cares!

It was a swimsuit miracle!

At the counter, Brittany rang up the suit and an amount appeared on the cash register.

BAAAAHH!

I guess miracles weren't cheap.

At home I tried on my suit for Quincey.

"That magic suit looks really good on you," she said. Then, she looked at the price tag. "Wow, that's pricey."

I nodded, unable to respond.

This suit was not designed for talking and wearing.

"You know," Quincey added. "It probably would have been easier to just lose ten pounds."

I wanted to respond with a snarky comment, but "I...uh...uh...uh..." was all I could utter.

And then it dawned on me where those ten pounds went.

They had been sucked internally and were currently crushing vital organs.

I looked at myself in the mirror.

Totally worth it.

Dough is Me

Before the holidays, I was a relatively healthy individual.

But after a season of decadence, I was 90 percent sugar and alcohol. My bones were toffee, my organs were cookie dough, and Cabernet coursed through my veins.

If you're a cannibal, I'm your gal.

On January 3, my doughy physique entered the gym.

For thirty minutes, I wheezed my way through a workout.

"First time here?" The perky young gal next to me asked.

If only I had the strength to smack her.

Vowing never to return, I headed for the exit.

Instead, I was stopped by Muscles, the gym manager. Like a predator that could detect fear, Muscles could sniff out a high BMI. "How would you like to be part of our 2020 Fitness Challenge?" he asked.

If only I had the agility to escape.

Muscles moved quickly. Within five minutes, I handed over my credit card to pay for three months of weekly weigh-ins. I tried to explain that my pride wasn't for sale, but the $75 receipt said otherwise.

Muscles took me into his office. "You can take off your shoes," he said.

"And?" I asked.

"Step on the scale," he added.

Was he insane?

I began mentally calculating the extra weight I was carrying: t-shirt, sports bra, leggings, socks, scrunchie…

Did he want me to cry?

I should take everything off and make him cry.

Muscles guided me to the scale. I tried to fight him, but he was too strong (hence the name). In a final act of defiance, I flung my scrunchie across the room, no doubt sparing me crucial ounces.

But it couldn't spare me from the pain I was about to endure as Muscles read those numbers aloud.

"AAAAAH!!!"

Good Lord, those are second trimester numbers.

Maybe I'm pregnant?

Except, I'm fifty-three, so maybe not.

The fun continued with the body fat measuring.

"Is this where you put clamps on my flab?" I asked.

"No clamps," Muscles promised. "We use the Fit3D scanning machine."

Muscles led me to a circular metal platform and instructed me to grasp the handles. After a series of beeps, the machine slowly rotated me in a clockwise fashion, like a rotisserie chicken.

It was the most fun I had all day.

You know what wasn't fun?

The email I received from Muscles the following day.

I opened it, expecting an apology letter.

Instead, Muscles had sent me a list of all my measurements, also known as hate mail.

I couldn't believe what I was reading.

Surely, that was a typo.

Did they measure my waist twice?

Did the highest BMI win?

But the true horror was yet to come.

Scrolling down, I discovered a live image similar to what you might see in a futuristic sci-fi movie. You know, where they show the hologram of a body rotating on a high-tech grid? In the movies, the body is always tall, sleek, and ready for battle.

The image he sent was short, doughy, and ready for dessert.

How dare Muscles send such an unflattering picture!

I'm going to march right down to that gym and give him a piece of my mind!

If only I had the endurance.

White Dress Bod

Some women look wonderful in a white dress. Their skin is flawless, their curves appear in just the right places, and everything seems to fit seamlessly into that perfect white package.

And then there are the rest of us.

For the most part, this doesn't cause an emotional toll. It's just hard to be around White Dress Bod people.

Me: That dress looks great on you.

White Dress Bod Friend: Thanks. You can borrow it anytime.

Me: I don't think so.

White Dress Bod Friend: Why not?

I shake my head. It's like veterans trying to explain war to civilians.

Last week, I got invited to a Black Tie/White Dress event. After some sobbing and mild hysteria, I headed to the mall. I gave myself a pep talk on the way.

Today is your day!

You're off to find dresses, whiter than white.

You'll be beautiful, stunning,

They'll fit you just right!

No frets, No fears,

No time for tears,

Your white dress is waiting,

Today is your day!

My Dr. Seuss themed speech was so inspiring that I practically skipped into Macy's and headed for the dress department.

That's when I came face to face with the six-foot, sixteen-inch waist mannequin, clad in a sleek white dress. I fought my natural urge to rip off one of her plastic limbs and beat her to death with it. Instead, I picked out a slew of white dresses, reassuring myself that one of these was bound to be a winner. Forget the fact that the previous 800 white dresses I've tried on in my life looked horrendous.

Today was different.

Once in the dressing room, I discarded my T-shirt and jeans and took the first white dress off the hanger. After unzipping the dress, I tentatively stepped one foot at a time into the garment. So far, so good.

I pulled the material up. It fit nicely around my middle. Not too snug. My heart raced.

Today is the day!

I slipped the right, then left arm in. At this point, the dress still resembled the one that was on the mannequin. I sucked in a little, then a lot, just to give the dress a fighting chance. I closed my eyes as I ran my fingers over the material. It felt smooth.

This IS the day!

I took one more deep breath, and…

This was NOT the day!

It was horrifying, but like a train wreck, I couldn't look away!

What happened to the dress on the mannequin? And where did all these lumps come from? And how many pounds does the mirror add?

I brushed away a rejection tear. They really should stock dressing rooms with tissues, or Prozac, or better yet, inspirational speakers.

Doggone it, you're good enough, you're smart enough, and people like you!

Maybe I just need to look at it from a different angle. I turned sideways.

Not bad for a woman in her second trimester.

Perhaps from the back?

Hello, back fat.

I turned back around, praying for a miraculous improvement. If only it was a vegetable-themed party, I could go as mashed potatoes.

The next twelve dresses were equally horrifying.

I fled the white carnage in the dressing room and ran through the store, once again, coming face to face with my nemesis.

The smooth white dress, the smug smile, it was more than I could take. The rest was just a blur of flailing plastic limbs and verbal assaults.

That mannequin really had a mouth on her.

So here I sit in a county booking room, facing Penal Code charges 594 and waiting for my husband to post bail. My hands are cuffed and like a common criminal, I'm wearing the orange jumpsuit.

"It's just that I had tried on so many white dresses," I tell the woman officer who leads me out of the room.

She nods.

She understands.

Walking down the hall, I catch a glimpse of myself in the mirror, and it hits me.

I look really good in orange!

Mother Tucker

Remember when you were a kid, how excited you were to be in a photo? You enthusiastically jumped in, front and center! "Cheese!"

Ah, the innocence of youth.

But now that we are all older and wiser, this does NOT happen. Sure, we still smile and say "Cheese" (unless we're lactose intolerant), but front and center?

No way, Jose.

It was about ten years ago when I saw myself in a group photo, FRONT AND CENTER.

Yikes!

Now, this shouldn't be surprising because, with each passing year, the camera adds several pounds.

Also known as $C + \uparrow y = \uparrow p$

It's just math, people.

Now that I was aware of this scary math, I decided to do something about it.

(No, I did not go on a diet.)

The next time I was in a group picture, I subtly slid behind the person next to me, and *voila!* I looked 10 pounds lighter.

It's called "tucking," and tucking will take off a good ten, twenty, fifty pounds.

$T = -p$

Again, math.

So, now every time I take a picture, I tuck.

Of course, in order to be a tucker (or in my case, a Mother Tucker), there must be a "tuckee."

And that's where Steve, comes in.

He knows when our picture is being taken, he must immediately take his place in front of me, so that I can slither behind until I'm practically non-existent.

"Hey, why do I look so huge, and you look so tiny?" He sighed, scrutinizing a recent photo.

I shrugged. "That's weird."

However, Steve can't complain because it's in our vows. After loving and before cherishing, there was definitely talk of tucking.

Sorry, men, I know this seems sexist, but it's your job.

(Except for our friends, Linda and Bill. Bill is the tucker in that relationship.)

I don't know what kind of crazy vows they took.

And it's not just Steve who acts as my tuckee.

My whole family knows when it's picture time, this mother be tuckin'!

Unfortunately, some people are getting tired of my antics.

"Why do you always get to be the tucker?" my friend Lorraine asked recently.

"Well, only one of us can tuck at a time," I explained as I subtly nestled behind her. "How about I tuck this picture, and then you can tuck in the next?"

(Sidenote: There was no next picture.)

Of course, even when I tuck, I'm not always pleased with the picture. (Again, camera's fault.)

However, I've learned, the more I tuck and the farther I am from the camera, the better I look.

$T + D = F$

(D = Distance. F, of course, stands for Fabulous.)

Was I the only one who paid attention in math?

I've gotten to the point where I'm so good at tucking that you can't even see my body anymore.

I'm merely a speck in the upper righthand corner.

Basically, a floating head.

A fabulous floating head.

Thelma and Louise and Louise

A million years ago, when we were in our 30s, my girlfriends and I started going on Girls' Weekends. It didn't matter where we went. The point was we were gone.

A weekend away from toddlers, housework, and husbands.

Three friends on an adventure.

Like Thelma and Louise and Louise.

But with a happier ending.

Back then, our weekends usually took place in Palms Springs or Vegas.

It was a weekend tanning by the pool, where it was a balmy 115 degrees.

At night, we'd spend hours doing our makeup and selecting the perfect mini-skirt and four-inch heels.

Thelma, our resident hair stylist, did our hair.

Then out on the town we went.

Happy hour margaritas, a fancy dinner, and then dancing to '80s music at a hip club.

Sometimes, we'd strike up a conversation with a handsome man.

But enough about our waiter.

Yep, we were young and reckless back then, staying out until the wee hours of the morning.

Then our 40s hit.

Since we were no longer interested in becoming human raisins, Vegas and Palm Springs were out.

Instead, we traveled to quaint beach towns, like La Jolla or Santa Barbara.

We spent lazy days soaking up rays on soft, white sands.

Under a huge umbrella, while wearing ginormous hats, we slathered SPF3,000 sunscreen on any exposed skin.

It's called harmful ultraviolet rays, people.

At night, we still got dolled up, applying makeup before deciding on the perfect capris and sandals with a spunky, but supportive wedge.

Thelma, always the stylist, still did our hair.

But while looking at the menu before we left, one of us (me) would say, "You know this place delivers."

Louise would sigh. "But we just got dressed."

Three Hannibals out (in) on the town.

So, we'd take a selfie (or whatever it was called fifteen years ago) to capture the illusion we were three wild women all dressed up and out on the town.

Then we'd change into sweats, practice a little line-dancing in the room, and wait for our BBQ chicken salads to be delivered.

163

It was wild.

But if you think that was bonkers, let me introduce you to our current Girls' Weekend.

Now, in our 50s, we prefer a much different type of destination.

Any town that throws out the word, "sleepy" is a big draw.

Also, we'd like to be as far away from the sun as possible.

Is Jupiter open?

On our last Girls Weekend, we decided on a Northern California town called Carmel.

It promised to be a comatose cloud-covered weekend!

The fun started before we even arrived.

We stopped at a CVS because Thelma forgot her Menoquil. I mocked her for buying such a middle-aged product on what was supposed to be a wild weekend. But then, I realized I had left my reading glasses at home, and *dammit, I can't see a thing without my Costco 2.5 readers.*

Meanwhile, Louise had meandered into the pharmacy to check her blood pressure.

In line, I shook my head at my friends.

Look at us, with our hot flash pills and glasses and slightly elevated blood pressure.

I threw in a few minis of Fireball.

Fortunately, the weekend took a turn for the better because Louise had brought a whole bag of…

Succulents!

We spent Saturday afternoon making succulent planters.

Nothing says "Wild Weekend" like porous soil and drought- resistant plants.

A few hours later, it was time to get ready for our Saturday night shenanigans.

Hair was styled, makeup applied, and we all picked out the perfect pajamas and supportive slippers.

Plantar fasciitis is no joke!

Also, you gotta be comfy when you're playing Scrabble and watching *Doc Martin.*

Then we had shots of Fireball (which is basically a liquid hot flash, but more fun) and Thelma slurred, "We're so blessed to have each other."

Did she just say *blessed*?

We're not in church, Thelma.

But she was right.

"I wonder what our Girls' Weekends will be like when we're in our 60s," Louise said.

I imagine pretty wild.

Chapter 8 - Midlife Mysteries

Where are all my forks? Why doesn't anyone respect the Stat?
Which bear is most likely to eat me?

Forksgiving

This Thanksgiving, I reflected on all the things I was thankful for.

Family, food, shelter…

And forks!

You heard me right.

Forks.

You see, for many years now, we've struggled to keep forks in the house.

A roof over our head?

No problem.

But forks in the utensil drawer?

Problem.

Almost daily a new fork went AWOL.

"WHERE ARE ALL MY FORKS?!" I screamed at my barren utensil drawer.

I checked other drawers, the dishwasher, the trash can.

It was a mystery.

Who is taking all my forks? Is it the same person who's stealing my reading glasses? (Don't even get me started on *that!*)

During Covid was when the forks began to vanish, and since Quincey, Colby, and Parker were all living here at the time, they were all suspects.

167

"Do you guys know where the forks are?" I'd ask those three rascals.

"Mom, shh, we're watching *Tiger King*," Parker would answer.

Even after they all moved out, forks continued to disappear at an alarming rate.

Every once in a while, Quincey would show up at our house to return a runaway (abducted) fork. "Sorry, Mom, I accidentally took this one home the other day."

If she "accidentally" took that one home, how many others are "accidentally" living in her new house?

So obviously, I did what any sane person would do.

I went to her house and conducted a thorough investigation.

Hey, Fork, hey, little Forky-Fork…

I went room to room.

"WE DON'T HAVE YOUR FORKS!" Quincey hollered.

Now, you're probably thinking, *hey, Ding Dong, why don't you just buy more?*

That was the plan.

Especially after last year's Thanksgiving fiasco when there weren't enough forks to go around.

Correction: enough *good* forks.

"Why is my fork so small?" our daughter Parker said, holding up a cocktail fork.

"You got the teeny, tiny fork," I said. "It forces you to take teeny, tiny bites and you don't eat as fast. You're welcome."

"Why is my fork so big?" Colby asked, holding up a utensil roughly the size of a pitchfork.

"Wow, you can fit your entire meal *and* dessert on that fork! Lucky!"

My husband examined his jagged fork, also known as Garbage Disposal Fork.

"Eat carefully," I whispered.

The next day I went on Amazon.

I sang myself a catchy tune to help me stay on track, *Forks, forks, forks, I definitely need forks.*

But do you know what else I needed?

Purely Elizabeth Pumpkin Spice Granola.

Click.

This happened quite a few times because, well, buying forks is boring.

You know what's not boring?

A stuffed animal ducky for my granddaughter, Holland. When you unzipped the butt, five little ducklings appeared.

Click.

But wait, didn't I need something else?

I shrugged.

It probably wasn't important.

This past September, I smartened up

Realizing I was incapable of purchasing my own forks, I decided to delegate.

"Forks," I told my friends when they asked what I wanted for my birthday.

"Forks?" Julie asked.

"Forks," I confirmed.

And that's what I got.

A big box of shiny forks.

Which is why Thanksgiving was such a hit this year.

No more B.Y.O.F.

Or *you're fine, just eat your turkey with your spoon.*

And our guests didn't get just one fork.

They were presented with a whole army of forks.

"That's your turkey fork, and that's your mashed potato fork, and here's your stuffing fork."

When it came time to cut the apple and pumpkin pies, each guest was awarded with yet another fork.

My fork runneth over!

A few minutes later, Quincey walked out of the kitchen holding a pie in each hand. "Mom, why don't you have any spatulas?"

I sighed.

Next year.

I'm definitely buying spatulas.

Papyru$

Yesterday, I bought a Papyrus card.

So, obviously, I can't pay my mortgage this month.

Seriously, these cards are expensive.

I can't give you an exact amount because there was no price on the back.

I guess these cards are "Market Price."

Like lobster.

But without the butter.

Anybody else hungry?

Now to be fair, the cards are beautiful.

It's not just folder paper with some sentiment scribbled upon it.

The card is made from papyrus (hence, the name).

The material, papyrus, has been used since ancient times for record keeping and important transactions, like the sale of a donkey.

I'd love to buy a donkey, but I just spent all my shekels on a card.

And it's not just what the card is made of, it's what is on it.

Many of them have beautiful flowers embossed on the front.

Based on the cost, I'm thinking these flowers are from the Garden of Eden.

Also, Papyrus cards come with a small note in the envelope.

That's the deed to your card.

However, the deed also includes information about hummingbirds.

Maybe Papyrus is really a front for GoFundMyHummingbird.

Which I would totally support.

Unless they're attaching actual hummingbirds to the card.

That's not cool.

Regardless, just know that if I sent you a papyrus card…

I'm homeless now.

But you're worth it.

Pillow Talk

Steve and I have eleven pillows on our bed right now.

Once upon a time, we had two pillows.

This is my pillow.

That is your pillow.

Good night.

Those were simpler times.

Over time, the pillows multiplied.

Two turned into four, and four into eight, and so on.

It was like Noah's Ark, with fertile pillows.

At one point I thought maybe I should thin the pillow herd, but thank goodness I didn't.

I have since discovered that I require no less than nine pillows for a good night's sleep.

Obviously, I need one pillow on which to rest my weary head.

This is my "Weary Head Pillow."

Except since I have heartburn, which requires me to elevate my head, it's best I sleep on multiple pillows.

I call the second pillow "Heartburn Pillow."

Just to clarify, the pillow doesn't give me heartburn. My poor food choices do.

The third one, "Menopause Pillow," not only adds extra elevation (I pretty much sleep sitting up), but it's the only pillow that stays cool all night long.

Unlike the other pillows that I have to flip continuously throughout the night (like some manic IHOP cook), this one never loses its cool.

God bless "Menopause Pillow!"

The next pillow I use is "Injury Pillow."

Correction: "Injury Pillows."

These pillows are strategically placed to combat all my ailments.

Currently, one is wedged under my stiff back (thanks a lot, pickleball),

one is between my knees (again, pickleball's fault), and the third is used

as a cushion for my pickleball elbow.

(Maybe I should stop playing pickleball.)

But, even with all these pillows, there's no way I'm getting any sleep, unless I have my two "Blackout Pillows." These are my lumpiest pillows, and I position the first one so that it sinks into my face, shielding my eyes. I then stack the second one on top, to ensure that I'm shrouded in complete darkness.

I like to feel like I'm sleeping in a coal mine.

I'm guessing by now, you're thinking, *Wow, this lady sure is a pillow hog! Does poor Steve even get one pillow?*

The answer is, *Yes!*

The ninth pillow, which is probably the most important pillow, is the

one that Steve and I share.

Adorable, right?

I refer to this pillow as the "Stop Breathing Pillow."

When Steve settles into his REM cycle, his breaths become deep, guttural sighs. These sighs then turn into dramatic exhales, which fill the room.

Basically, I'm sleeping with Darth Vader.

I try shushing him.

There are some gentle nudges and kicks.

Darth slumbers on.

This is when I lovingly place this pillow over his face.

"Stop breathing," I whisper.

Again, I cannot emphasize how tenderly I say this.

Fortunately, this usually does the trick.

After Steve fights off the pillow and the look of terror dissipates from his eyes, he settles back in. His breathing is now at a more acceptable level.

Like that of a hibernating bear.

That's when we finally both fall asleep.

Just the two of us.

And our eleven pillows.

The Stat

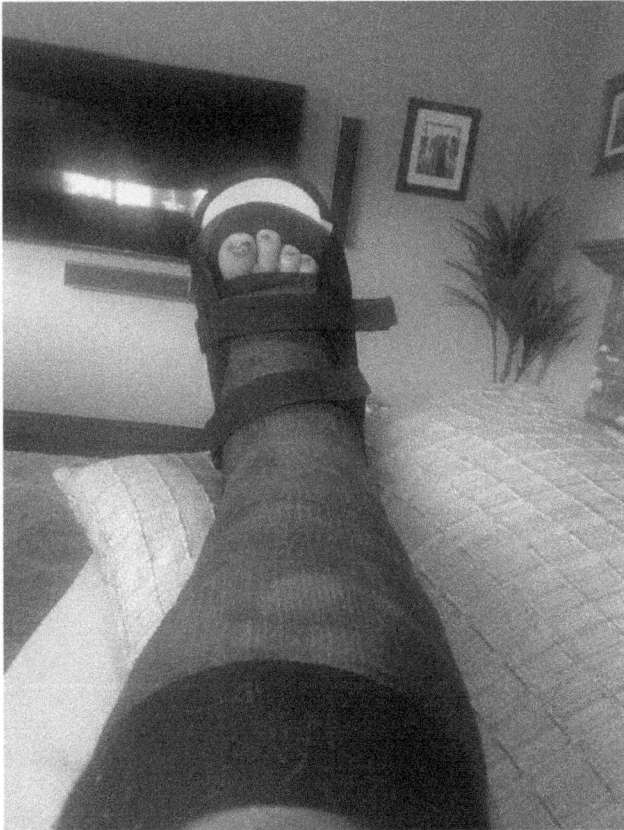

I'd love a new ankle, STAT!

The day after my fall, I saw my doctor. Examining my bruised and swollen ankle, he shook his head and said, "We need to get you X-rays. Tell them you need these STAT!"

My eyes grew wide.

I was going to be just like on TV.

Nurse, get this woman a new ankle, STAT!

Ten minutes later, I hobbled enthusiastically into the lab and handed the receptionist my paperwork, "The doctor says he needs this...STAT!"

The receptionist took my paperwork. "Okay, have a seat."

I took a seat, but I didn't get too comfy because as I may have mentioned, my X-rays were STAT!

In the next fifteen minutes, three other people were called.

"Are your X-rays, stat, too?" I whispered to the woman leaving the room.

She ignored me.

I returned to the front desk. "Um, sorry to bother you, but I have X-rays that are stat," I explained.

"We'll get to you when we can," she said.

THAT'S LIKE THE OPPOSITE OF STAT!

More names were called. I caught the eye of the receptionist. "Stat," I mouthed as a gentle reminder.

Nothing!

Forty-five stat-less minutes later, my name was called. The technician led me into the room at a brisk pace.

Now you decide to move fast!

Once in the x-ray room, she had me sit on a table and told me to hold still.

I didn't bother telling her that my X-rays were stat.

I did, however, ask for a lead apron since she didn't give me one.

What sort of operation are you running, Lady?

She sighed and half-heartedly threw me an apron.

I shook my head, visibly upset.

She probably thought I was mad about being radiated.

But all I could think was, *why don't they respect the STAT?*

Meals on Wheels

The month prior to our Alaskan vacation, Google began sending me grizzly (no pun intended) bear stories.

These were not warm and fuzzy anecdotes, like *Bear and Ranger Share Pot of Honey.*

It was more: *Hiker Loses Limb After Bear Mauling.*

Apparently, Google thinks I have a dark side.

(I do.)

I shared my concerns with my husband Steve and friends, Lorraine and Nick, as we began our bike ride along the Alaskan coast.

Scanning the forest adjacent to the trail, I asked, "What if we see a bear?"

"You make yourself big," Steve said.

"You play dead," Nick said.

"If it's a brown bear, play dead," Steve elaborated. "Black bear, be big."

"How big?" I asked, sizing up my own 5'3" frame.

"Just stand tall, wave your arms, and make a lot of noise," Steve added.

"But no high-pitched screaming," Nick said.

I'm fairly sure if I run into a bear, my voice will be high.

Also, my pants may be wet.

"Talk to the bear in calm tones," Nick added.

"What should I talk to the bear about?" I asked.

"Pretty much anything," Nick answered.

"Just not religion or politics," I said.

"Also, black bears aren't always black," Nick said. "Sometimes they're brown."

Whoa, Whoa, WHAT?!

"So how do I know if it's a real black bear, or a black bear that's identifying as a brown bear?" I asked.

"By the hump."

"And the ears."

Steve and Nick conducted a mini bear hump and ear tutorial.

In case you missed the tutorial: Brown bears have smaller ears and a hump on their back.

Also, if their ears go back, they're about to charge, and you're in a wee bit of trouble.

"And don't ever get between a mama bear and her cub," Lorraine added.

Duh.

It was a lot of information, but in summary…

Black bear, big,

Brown bear, dead,

Don't get between,

Mama and her cub.

(I think I have the makings for an adorable, albeit disturbing, children's book.)

"Either way, the bear probably won't get all of us," I said.

I proceeded to share a recent story of how a Grizzly had attacked four hikers.

Three got away.

I sized up my middle-aged, injury-riddled bunch.

I liked my chances.

For sixteen miles, we saw nothing but lush greenery, calm waters, and puffy clouds.

On Mile 17, Lorraine and I (who were slightly ahead of our husbands) turned a blind corner, and...

Thirty feet in front of us...

Smack in the middle of the trail...

Dark fur, huge paws, mammoth claws...

GRRRRRRR!

I slammed on my brakes, praying I would stop without flying over the handlebars and catapulting myself into the bear.

What's the etiquette if you crash into a bear?

Thankfully, I screeched to a halt and jumped off the bike just in time.

With trembling hands, I laid my bike on the side of the trail.

Slowly, I lifted my eyes.

My mind started racing...*Was it okay to look directly at the bear?*

Or like a gorilla, do I avoid eye contact?

Or should I give it a subtle wink, like, Hey, Bear, we're all good. Nothing to eat here.

My heart pounded in my ears as I stood motionless, taking in this majestic creature.

The bear sat in the middle of the trail, gnawing on greenery.

Was he a vegetarian?

181

Excellent!

I seemed to recall from Steve's seminar that black bears *are* vegetarians, but was *this* a black bear?

Unfortunately, I'm slightly color blind so I couldn't tell you the exact color.

I could, however, tell you the size...

GINORMOUS!

RUN, RUN, RUN, I screamed to myself.

"Do NOT run!" Lorraine read my mind. "And don't turn your back on it!"

The bear continued to chomp on shrubbery.

That's it, spoil your appetite. Good bear.

My heart raced. I turned to Lorraine for words of comfort.

"Do you want to take a picture?" she asked.

No. I want to live.

I edged backwards, forcing myself not to bolt.

Lorraine just stood, enjoying the view.

How could she be so calm?

But then I remembered.

Lorraine was voted "Most Calm, Cool and Collected," Class of 1984.

(Fellow Trojans, you voted correctly.)

"Can we get out of here?" I whimpered, turning my back on the bear.

(I should have been voted "Least Likely to Follow Directions.")

Lorraine nodded and backpedaled, keeping her eye on the bear.

"We're going to be fine," Lorraine reassured me. "But remember, if he attacks, lie on your stomach so he can't get your organs,"

Goodbye Lorraine, it's been nice knowing you!

Seconds later, Steve and Nick appeared on the path.

I planted myself in the middle of the trail and raised my hand as if I were directing traffic.

"Stop!" I commanded. "There's a bear!"

WHOOSH!

That was the sound of the two of them riding past me.

"Cool!" Nick said, as he pedaled towards the bear.

"Awesome," Steve added, as he jumped off the bike and began videotaping.

And the rest is history.

One day, a group of slightly injured, fairly misguided, bear-loving friends went on a bike ride and encountered a bear.

And lived to tell about it.

Take that, Google.

Chapter 9 - I Love You an Unhealthy Amount

I ~~may~~ have a problem.

Dear Wordle

Dear Wordle,

My friend introduced me to you yesterday. It was love at first word. I'm hoping you feel the same way.

Dear Wordle,

It's been a week and you're all I think of. Before I even open my eyes in the morning, I whisper your name, "Wordle."

What am I doing?

You've made it clear that this is an open relationship.

I'm such a fool.

Dear Wordle,

Everyone had trouble with "CYNIC," but not me. I love that we both share an affinity for consonant clusters. Isn't that what a healthy relationship is based on?

Dear Wordle,

"TACIT?"

I think we're about to have our first fight.

Dear Wordle,

Yesterday, I guessed "AROMA" on the second round, and you told me I was "Magnificent!" I was on cloud nine until my neighbor, Connie, said you told her she was also "Magnificent."

How many others did you say that to?

Never mind, I don't want to know.

Dear Wordle,

When you say, "Great," you and I both know that five rounds are *not* great. I can sense the rolling of the eyes, the sarcastic tone. I thought our relationship was built on honesty. I guess I was wrong.

Dear Wordle,

I told my therapist about you and how I was afraid I might be in a codependent relationship.

My therapist corrected me. "Dependent. You're in a dependent relationship."

Dear Wordle,

Connie got "THEIR" on the first try and she's telling everyone that you said she's a "Genius." She thinks she's better than me.

Thanks a lot, Wordle.

Dear Wordle,

I dreamed about you last night. In the dream, the adjective "Splendid" had been changed to "Mediocre," and "Great" was now "Disappointing." I think the dream signifies that we need more transparency. Also, I may be obsessed with you.

PS: Do you dream about me?

Dear Wordle,

"SHAWL?!" You just did "SHALL" three days ago.

It feels as if I'm the only one working in this relationship.

Dear Wordle,

As you know, Connie uses the same two starter words every day, while I'm always coming up with new words to keep our relationship F-R-E-S-H! But she's doing better than I am! Why are you rewarding laziness? I thought we shared the same values.

Dear Wordle,

I guessed "MORAY" instead of "FORAY." It's like you want to hurt me.

Dear Wordle,

Tomorrow is our two-month anniversary. It's been a long time since I was "Magnificent," and I've never been "Genius," so maybe you can T-H-I-N-K about a special word for me tomorrow.

Dear Wordle,

Oh, the SHAME!

I can't believe that's what you chose for our anniversary word. It's clear that you're obviously ashamed of me. Or you want to shame me. Or our relationship is filled with shame.

As I kept plugging in words (Shade, Shake, Shape) like some simpleton, I thought to myself, surely you wouldn't WordleShame me.

But apparently our 59 days together meant nothing.

It's over, Wordle.

I deserve more.

Dear Quordle…

Hey, Batter Batter

Last Sunday, I made chocolate chip cookies for a friend's party.

Mix, mix, mix.

Whisk, whisk, whisk.

Sample, sample, sample.

Delicious!

I put the first batch in the oven, and then ate a spoonful.

And three more.

Just to be sure.

Once all the cookies were in the oven, I finished off the batter, because, well, "No batter left behind."

"Hey, good looking," I said, winking at my cookies, through the oven glass.

Clearly, I was hopped up on batter.

An hour later, I pulled the last batch out of the oven and did a quick inventory.

The liars at Nestle said the recipe would make forty-eight cookies, but I only counted thirty-three.

And that's when I started to sweat.

At first, I thought it was because the kitchen was hot.

However, this sweating was like how one might feel after eating too much bacon.

Do not pretend you don't know what I'm talking about.

We've all had the "bacon sweats."

But this was worse.

My head throbbed.

My stomach churned.

"I don't feel so well," I told Steve, running out of the room.

I won't go into detail, because...

Yuck.

Let's just say, two hours later, with no relief in sight, I lay on the bathroom tile, wailing, "Make...It...Stop!"

Steve rubbed my back.

"I...think...I...need...to...go...to...Urgent...Care," I stammered, in between moans and groans.

I know there are people who suffer in silence, but my rule is, if I'm going to suffer, we're all going to suffer.

Steve helped me downstairs and, somehow, I made my way into the passenger's seat.

Sweaty and nauseous, I clung to my barf bowl, as if it were a life preserver.

Steve looked at me in all my splendor.

"Is that what you're wearing?" he asked, backing down our driveway.

Ratty t-shirt, boxer shorts, robe.

If that's not "Urgent Care" attire, I don't know what is.

(Also known as, "Smart Casual.")

He did have a point, though.

My maroon robe totally clashed with my red bowl.

Honestly though, I've never been one to accessorize.

Steve raced down our street, through the neighborhood, and accelerated onto the freeway.

"Please…go…faster!" I whimpered.

70 mph!

80 mph!

And then just as he hit 85 mph…

Flashing lights appeared in the rear-view mirror.

Steve slammed on the brakes and veered to the side of the road.

The officer approached our window. "License and registration," he said.

This reminded me of twenty-four years earlier, when we got pulled over on the way to the hospital to deliver Parker.

(Just to be clear, *we* didn't deliver Parker. The doctors delivered Parker.)

Steve had used the phrase, "Officer, my wife is with baby," and he let us go.

Unfortunately, that wouldn't work today, so Steve said the next best thing.

"Officer, my wife is with batter."

I'm not sure if the officer completely understood, but after eyeing the bowl in my lap, we were on our way.

Ten minutes later, Steve checked me into Exer Urgent Care.

"My wife had too much batter," he told the receptionist.

"Batter?" the woman asked.

"Batter," Steve confirmed.

The woman raised an eyebrow.

Am I the only one overdosing on cookie dough?

In the examining room, we had a similar reaction from Nurse John, who scrunched his face as he read the notes. "So, basically, you ate a large quantity of cookie batter?" he asked.

Sheesh, have these people never made cookies before?!

While Nurse John checked my blood pressure, he joked with me, trying to make me feel better. He had an excellent bedside manner and if I weren't so vomity, I feel like we could have exchanged some witty repartee.

Next time, I promise, they'll be less barfing, more banter.

A few minutes later, the doctor appeared and after checking my chart, she turned to Nurse John. "Batter?" she mouthed.

"Batter," he nodded.

She scratched her head.

Lady, you went to medical school. I've got to believe there was a rotation on "batter."

"Based on the amount of batter you consumed, how many cookies do you think it was equivalent to?"

Fifteen.

"Two, maybe three," I said.

"Hmm," she said.

Clearly, I was lying right through my dough hole.

After jotting down more info, the doctor said, "We're going to give you a shot of Zofran, stat!"

Usually, when the doctors say "Stat," it's anything but!

However, at Exer Urgent Care, *STAT MEANS STAT!*

Another nurse appeared (STAT) and gave me a shot in the ass of Zofran.

It was the highlight of my day.

Besides eating all that delicious cookie dough.

Then, Nurse John administered an IV of fluids, and I'm not sure what these fluids were (Dr. Pepper?), but an hour later, I walked out of the room, feeling almost normal.

"How are you doing, hon?" Steve asked, putting his arm around me.

"Batter now," I joked.

Look at me, throwing out a well-placed pun.

If only Nurse John could see me now.

That night, my friend, Luann called to check up on me.

I updated her on the batter fiasco, and she informed me that, according to her research, one in 20,000 eggs have salmonella, and there's a chance I ate that egg today.

What are the odds?

Oh, yeah, one in 20,000.

That week, I did my own investigating and found a ton of articles about the dangers of ingesting cookie dough.

Most of the articles started with, "What to do if your eight-year-old eats too much batter…"

What about your 55-year-old?

Ageism, am I right?

In the end, though, there were silver linings.

One of which was that I now have a new favorite medical facility.

Exer Urgent Care, I'm giving you ★★★★★!

Even though you only gave me ★★.

("Pukey, poorly dressed, lackluster personality…")

However, the biggest takeaway from all of this was the lesson I learned:

The next time I make cookies and that little voice inside of me whispers, "Hey, Batter Batter…"

I will just respond with, "No Batter, No Batter, No Batter…"

Lost and Found

On the side of a deserted farm road, behind a clump of weeds was where we found him. To this day, I don't know who left him or how he got there.

It was Quincey who spotted him. "Did you see that?" she asked.

I pulled to the side and looked back, my eyes following her gaze. Barely visible in the brown grass, he lay.

Round.

Purple.

Still.

Quincey got out of the car and ran towards him. She pulled him out of the ditch and hoisted him over her head as she raced back to the car. She placed him in the back seat.

We drove away.

"How do you think he got there?" she asked.

"I have no idea."

That week, when my friends came over to my house for our weekly boot camp, they were equally mystified.

Lisa wrapped her arms around his enormous middle. "He's a big boy."

Julie shook her head. "Who leaves a perfectly good exercise ball on the side of the road?"

That was the mystery.

Was he flung from a moving vehicle?

Escaping a sadistic gym owner?

Or did an open garage and a strong breeze lead him to his destiny?

"Well, he's ours now," I said.

And that's how Big Purple Ball came into our lives. Sure, we had plenty of other exercise equipment, but this one was special. Over time, when the weights became worn, the bands broke, and the exercise balls deflated, Big Purple Ball remained his pristine, perfect self.

Big Purple Ball was part of our workouts for six months. Then one Thursday, while setting out equipment, Big Purple Ball wasn't in his usual spot. *Hmmm.*

I searched the garage, inside the house, the backyard.

Nothing.

Big Purple Ball had many talents, but hiding wasn't one of them.

He's got to be here somewhere.

The following week, he was still missing.

My friends and I discussed Big Purple Ball's sudden disappearance while jumping rope on the driveway.

"He probably rolled away," Julie said.

Lisa added, "And unfortunately, you live on a hill."

If Big Purple Ball escaped down the driveway, it was all downhill after that. He may have literally rolled out of our lives forever.

All I could think was…

Why Purple Ball, why?

We gave you a good home.

And yes, moms aren't supposed to have favorites, but clearly you were.

I spent several afternoons gazing in garages, combing bushes, peeking through fences.

Nothing.

But somehow, I felt he was close. I contemplated putting up a sign:

Why not?

That Lost Kitten sign has been posted to our mailbox for weeks.

Who's to say your stupid kitten is more important than my Big Purple Ball?

I'm sorry, your kitten isn't stupid. I'm lashing out.

A month later, while walking my dog, it happened.

Several houses down, in an open garage, between a set of golf clubs and a tub of beach toys, he sat.

BIG PURPLE BALL!

Maybe it's not him. There are others that resemble him. I've seen his siblings at Walmart, Dick's, 24-hourFitness.

I made my way up their driveway, getting a closer look.

It was HIM.

I didn't feel right just taking him, so I continued walking. I practiced what I would say when I returned.

Ten minutes later, I headed back up my street. I stopped in front of the kidnapper's house, prepared to take back what was rightfully mine.

The garage door was now closed.

That's okay, I'll be back.

And I was, several times. The garage door was often open, but Big Purple Ball was nowhere in sight.

I guess I could have just asked, but there's something about a middle-aged woman knocking on a stranger's door and saying, "I want my ball back," that screamed *Dateline Special*.

Months went by, the garage door remained open, kids played in the front yard, but Big Purple Ball was MIA.

It wasn't until early December that I got my first lead.

I was teaching PE at the local elementary school, when a kid said to me, "I think you live on my street."

I studied the freckled, sandy-haired boy. "What's your name?"

"Joey," he answered.

And then I knew.

Joey lived in the house.

Joey had my ball.

"Um Joey," I said. "This is going to sound weird, but a few months ago, did you happen to find a big purple ball?"

His eyes got big. "Yeah, we got it out of our neighbor's trash."

And just like that, mystery solved. Big Purple Ball had rolled down the street (accidental or premeditated, we'll never know) and ended up in a neighbor's yard. Neighbor had no need for Big Purple Ball and placed him in trash. Joey's family took him out of trash and gave Big Purple Ball a new home.

"It's actually my ball," I told Joey.

"Okay," Joey said, shrugging.

Okay?

Okay, you can have your ball back.

Or…

Okay, it's my ball now.

The bell rang and Joey was gone.

I didn't do anything for a few weeks. But one day, while stretching with the kids at PE, I whispered, "Psst, Joey, you still have my ball, right?"

"Yep," he said.

This Joey wasn't much of a talker.

"I guess I'll come by sometime and get it," I said.

"Okay," Joey said, then ran off to do his laps.

Three weeks later, I did.

It was over Christmas break, and Parker was home from college.

"Why do I have to go too?" she grumbled, as we headed down the street.

"With you there, it'll be less weird," I said.

"Trust me, it's still going to be weird," she said. "And you know there are stores that sell the same ball. I can buy you one."

I shook my head.

199

I wanted THIS ball.

My daughter rang the bell. I took a deep breath. The mom opened the door. After a nudge from my daughter, I cleared my throat and said what I rehearsed.

She smiled. "I'm sorry. Joey never mentioned that it was your ball."

Typical Joey.

"And unfortunately…"

Uh oh.

"We left the side gate open about a week ago, and I guess the ball just rolled away."

My ball rolled away?

My BALL?

MY BIG PURPLE BALL!

"I guess that ball really likes to travel," she added.

She had no idea.

I spent more time scouring the neighborhood, but I never did reunite with Big Purple Ball. Sometimes, on a deserted road, they'll be something purple and round in the distance, but when I get closer, I realize it's just an illusion.

My therapist is trying to find out what sort of deep-seated loss the ball represents.

But I keep telling her, "It was just a really good ball."

Jackpot!

Are you Chitin Me?

I have a lot of obsessions: Running, Wine, Running with Wine, Succulents, *The Bachelor* (do not judge me), and my most recent...

WWF.

No, not the World Wrestling Federation.

But thank you for thinking I could compete at that level.

WWF is *Words with Friends*.

Harmless, right?

Harmless like heroin.

I blame my friend, Linda, who visited last weekend.

During her stay, we played multiple Scrabble games.

The competition was fierce.

Think gladiators with wooden tiles.

"You should get *Words with Friends*," she suggested. "Then we could play each other."

Do I dare?

Oh, I dared.

On Sunday, I installed *Words with Friends* on my phone.

On Monday, I received my first notification: It's Your Turn!

LT (Linda) had challenged me to a game.

What a rush!

Over the next few days, LT and I played multiple games.

She threw down words like quad, oxide, and zigged.

I countered with blazer, capote, and loq.

But I was no match for this word whiz, who put down chitin for a triple word score.

Are you chitin me?!

Once the game was over, I received a notification: You Lost!

As if the all caps and exclamation point wasn't enough of a kicker, it was accompanied by LT's smiling face.

The folks at WWF are a sadistic bunch.

Maybe I should play someone easier.

Ethel57 and Junebugs64 invited me to play.

But it's not called *Words with Strangers*.

I continued to play LT.

Every time my phone pinged, I salivated like some Pavlovian dog.

You thought a gender reveal was exciting?

Try a word reveal!

On my screen, new letters appeared, accompanied by an upbeat xylophone tune. The bloopity-bloop sound seemed to say, *Go for that triple word score*!

Believe me, I tried.

Unfortunately, I keep ending up with all consonants.

Last game, I had v, y, g, b, l, t, z.

"I'd like to buy a vowel," I whispered into my phone.

Unfortunately, this game did not come with a Vanna.

Even more unfortunate, it's now Friday, and I've been on a five-day bender.

Plans canceled, housework neglected, stories unwritten.

I know what I must do.

Goodbye, LT.

Sayonara, Ethel 57.

It's been nice knowing you, Junebugs64.

But then…

Bloopity-bloop!

Well…

Just one more game.

Peppermint Patty

Eight weeks before we went on vacation, when I would be required to wear a bathing suit (sad face), I told myself, "You can do this! You can lose eight pounds in eight weeks!"

Eight days before we left, I reminded myself, "You can do this! You can lose ten pounds in eight days!"

The problem was that we had friends visiting the weekend before we left.

Forget sugar and carbs. Let's blame the friends.

"Hey, guys, who's feeling broccoli this weekend?" I asked the group.

(Spoiler Alert: No one.)

So, I went to Costco to pick out delicious snacks, like the gigantic container of Peanut M&Ms that beckoned me from Aisle 2. "I love you, too," I whispered, before fleeing. Trust me, I cannot be alone in a room with Peanut M&Ms.

Only one of us is coming out alive.

I scanned the aisle for something less tempting, which is how I ended up with a two-pound bag of White Chocolate Peppermint Pretzel Crisps.

Pretzels are too salty, peppermint is meh, and white chocolate is chocolate's less ethnic, boring cousin.

Folks, we have a winner.

With seven days and eleven pounds to lose, it was important that I stay the course.

It was all going so well until Saturday Night Skip-Bo (I don't need to tell you how wild our night was), when I broke out the WCPPC.

"Mm," everyone murmured. "These are good."

I rolled my eyes.

Seriously, how good could pretzels really be?

I took a bite.

I think the best way to describe it, without sounding weird, is like the beginning of a relationship, when you're so in love you can't keep your hands off each other.

I mean, technically, Pretzel Crisps don't have hands, so I guess I was the only handsy one.

Let's just say that we had a good weekend together.

And then a few good days after that.

But I knew I had to stop because I still had to lose thirteen pounds in four days, and I was becoming concerned that I might not achieve my goal.

That night, I handed Steve the bag. "You need to hide these from me."

He shrugged. "Okay."

Two hours later, I walked into the kitchen and there was the bag sitting on the counter.

Remind me not to play hide and seek

"Steve!" I yelled.

"What?" he asked, walking into the kitchen.

I finished chewing. "I told you to hide these."

"Oh, yeah, I forgot."

After we said our goodbyes, Steve took the WCPPC and hid them.

In his office.

I know this because that's where I found them the next day.

Trust me, I didn't want to find them, but then I thought of the saying, if *you love something, set it free. If it returns, it was meant to be.*

Obviously, we were meant to be together because there they were, on the top shelf, inside Steve's glass cabinet.

Apparently, Steve thinks I can't see through glass.

Sheesh, Buddy, I'm not that blind.

(Although I did recently apply a firming foot cream to my face. WHY DO THEY HAVE TO WRITE SO DAMN SMALL? IF I'M AT THE AGE THAT MY FACE REQUIRES FIRMING, USE A BIGGER FONT!)

I marched right into the other room and let Steve have it.

I may have also had a quick snack.

"You have to hide these, so I won't ever find them!" I told him.

And he did.

I mean, he *really* hid them.

Trust me, I looked everywhere.

But the good news is now I could lose those fifteen pounds in three days.

A few days later, on our tropical vacation 4,000 miles from home, I told our friends how WCPPC had completely derailed me. "If it wasn't for those damn pretzel chips, I'd have a beach bod right now," I said.

"You mean these pretzel chips?" my friend Lisa said, pointing to a bag on the counter.

Steve smiled.

I'm going to kill that guy.

Right after I have a quick snack.

Chapter 10 - If I Had a Big Book of Grievances, You Would Be in It

The names have been changed to protect the insufferable.

One ★ Swimming

Our whole family is big on reviews. Quincey doesn't so much as buy a toothbrush without making sure it has five stars. Steve doesn't frequent a restaurant unless it's Yelp approved.

I, on the other hand, rely on my gut.

While researching a swim instructor for my ten-month-old granddaughter, Holland, my gut told me to hire Sandy, a swim instructor I found on a mom's website.

Sandy had over twenty years of experience and was highly recommended.

She was recommended by herself, but still, I admired her confidence.

Sandy arrived for our lesson ten minutes early.

I introduced Sandy to Steve and Colby, who were both attempting to squeeze a squirming Holland into her swimsuit.

My husband handed Holland to Sandy, who smiled and babbled in Sandy's arms.

"We're going to have so much fun in the water," Sandy told Holland as we all headed outside.

Punctual AND Pleasant.

Who needs reviews when you have spot-on instincts, like me?

Sandy slowly made her way into the pool, placing Holland on the beach entrance, next to the steps. Holland splashed in the shallow water.

Steve gave me a smile that said, *you were right, Sandy is the best!*

I know.

Sandy turned to us. "I have the greatest pool toy."

We smiled.

"It's so much fun," she added.

We nodded.

"Babies absolutely love it," she said, staring off into space.

We followed her gaze.

Sandy sighed. "...But I forgot it."

Well, that's disappointing.

Sandy lifted Holland off the steps. "Which way is the shallow end?" she asked.

Nobody answered.

We were all thinking about that toy.

I know I was.

Finally, Steve pointed. "Towards the slide."

Sandy nodded and went the opposite direction.

One minute, Sandy was happily bouncing Holland in her arms.

The next moment, Sandy was treading water in the deep end, barely keeping her head above water, her eyes wide with fear.

"We're fine," she gurgled, holding Holland above her head like the Stanley Cup.

Steve raced to the edge of the pool, grabbed a flailing arm, and pulled the two of them back to safety.

Sandy coughed up chlorine.

Did we need a swim instructor for our swim instructor?

Back in the shallow end, Sandy gasped, "Oops, guess I went the wrong way."

Steve shot me a look.

Where did you find this lady?

I patted his shoulder.

Trust me. Sandy's ~~the best~~...okay.

Meanwhile, Sandy headed back down the steps. "How about we try going underwater?" she asked Holland. Then she turned to us. "It's very soothing, like being in the womb. Babies love it."

Dunk!

I can't speak for all babies, but this baby most certainly did *not* love it.

After that, it wasn't so much a swim lesson as it was grief counseling.

"I think she's had enough for today," Steve said, as he wrapped Holland in a towel.

Sandy sat on the edge of the steps. "Next week, I'll bring the toy," she smiled. "She's really going to love it."

I was torn.

I'm quite sure we wouldn't be inviting Sandy back, *but dammit, I'd love to see that toy.*

211

Sandy climbed out of the pool, and then stood, dripping on the cement. "I forgot a towel," she confessed.

We all looked at one another.

Who was this toy-less, towel-less wonder?

Steve, who was standing next to Colby, handed her a towel.

Sandy toweled off and then giving Steve and Colby a big smile, asked, "So have the two of you had Holland since birth?"

There was a very long, very awkward pause as we all registered what she was asking.

I don't care how progressive you are, no father-in-law and son-in-law want to be mistaken for life partners.

Let's just say Holland wasn't the only one traumatized that day.

We spent the next few minutes explaining to Sandy who went with who(m).

Sandy just smiled and nodded.

Then taking her (our) towel, she waved goodbye and that was the last we saw of Sandy.

Steve, Colby, and Holland all gave me the same look.

I nodded.

I know.

Reviews are important.

New Coyotes on the Block

For the past month, hungry coyotes have infested our quiet suburban neighborhood.

Thinking about going for a leisurely walk?

I'd suggest you bring your running shoes.

And a slower friend.

At first, neighbors reported just one coyote.

Then two, and soon three, and now, allegedly there's a pack.

Ravenous and menacing, they roam the neighborhoods.

Like teenagers.

(But not as frightening.)

Word on the street is that the coyotes venture out in the early evening to look for food.

Specifically, between 5 p.m. and 7 p.m.

Also known as "Happy Hour."

My mom and I encountered one a few blocks from my home.

We had just turned onto Shady Point Lane, and there he was.

About 100 yards away, poised in the middle of the sidewalk.

We stopped, frozen.

He moved towards us, sizing us up.

But not in a "Howdy, Neighbor" way.

More like a "You Look Delicious" way.

He picked up his pace.

"Run!" I yelled to my mom as I sprinted away, leaving her behind.

Hey, I never claimed to be a Marine.

(No mom Left Behind.)

Fortunately, two blocks away, she caught up with me.

That's when we ran into Marge, another neighbor.

Marge knew all about the coyotes.

"You know they're living in a house on Willowbrook Lane," she said.

"*In* the house?" I asked, raising an eyebrow.

She nodded.

"They moved in about a month ago," she added.

That was just plain ridiculous.

No coyote was going to buy right now.

I mean, with interest rates so high.

Later, we met up with another neighbor, Jill, who set us straight.

"They don't live *in* the house," Jill corrected. "They live *behind* the house."

In, behind…

Prepositions matter, Marge.

Howdy, Neighbor!

But I should have known all along, coyotes don't live in houses.

They're not bears.

Or pigs.

"When you say behind, do you mean in the backyard?" I asked.

Jill nodded.

"And does a family live *in* the house?" I asked.

Jill nodded again.

"A family of humans?"

"Yep."

"So, humans inside, coyotes outside," I said, summing up the situation.

Now, you're probably thinking, this poor family, what if they have dogs or small children?

I'm thinking, what's the situation for pool parties?

Are the coyotes inviting the humans, or are they being all exclusive?

Because if the humans have to just watch the coyotes play Marco Polo, that's gotta hurt.

Last week, my mom and I ran into the coyote again.

This time, he didn't seem the least bit interested in eating us.

Instead, he just nodded politely as we passed each other on the street.

I think he's starting to understand…

Neighbors don't eat neighbors.

However, they might not be our neighbors for long.

According to the coyote rumor mill, some people are plotting to get rid of the coyotes.

(That doesn't seem very neighborly.)

One mom suggested that we should start "hazing" the coyotes.

She had written on Facebook, "If you want to get rid of them, you need to haze them!"

Do coyotes even want to be in a fraternity?

But then someone else commented that we shouldn't haze the coyotes around their pups.

That made sense.

You don't bring your kid to a frat party.

Another mom reminded us that the coyotes were only interested in bunnies and squirrels.

Hello, what about roadrunners!

(BEEP, BEEP)

She also added that coyotes aren't that dangerous.

Except when they're blowing things up.

Sheesh.

It's like these moms had never even heard of Wiley.

But the latest scuttlebutt is that a new coyote family moved in last week.

Also, known as the New Coyotes on the Block.

(I wonder if they can sing.)

Yesterday, I saw the OG Coyotes and the New Coyotes hanging out at Peach Hill Park.

They were all howling at the moon.

So cliché.

Also, it was after 9 p.m., so *pipe down.*

Maybe they were planning something.

Perhaps a 4th of July Party?

If so, I hope I get an invite.

You know they'll have great fireworks.

The Big Cheese

For years I showed up at parties with my famous artichoke dip.

But then I learned that cheese boards were all the rage, and thought, *well, that sounds fun and easy!*

(Spoiler Alert: It's not. The cheese circuit is cutthroat. And I mean that *literally*. Show up with an overcooked Brie, and these women will cut you with a cheese spreader.)

A few years back I arrived at the neighborhood Christmas party with my first cheese plate, which consisted of cheddar cubes, salami slices, and Ritz crackers.

"A Lunchable…how nice," Chelsea, my neighbor and Soon-To-Be-Cheese-Rival, said, wiping Ritz dust from my shoulder.

This was followed by several of the women gasping in horror, "She cut her cheese in cubes!"

My ~~cheese plate~~ Lunchable was given to the dog.

Chelsea then unveiled her masterpiece: A charcuterie board filled with *triangular* cheeses, fancy meats, assorted nuts, fresh figs, and sesame crackers.

I vowed then and there that I would learn all about charcuterie.

Also, how to pronounce it.

The following year, I brought a spread of trendy cheese, prosciutto, and socially acceptable crackers.

"Manchego! Asiago! Gouda!" I introduced my star-studded cheese lineup.

The room went deathly quiet.

"Asiago without lemon curd?" Chelsea pointed a cheese spreader at me. "Do you even know about jam pairings?"

Those were fighting words.

"And where's the Havarti?" someone asked. "It's not a party without Havarti."

I smacked myself with my own Gouda.

The time had come to step up my cheese game.

Entering the 2019 party, I presented an assortment of well-aged cheeses with perfectly paired jams, surrounded by the finest accoutrements.

Oohs and aahs reverberated throughout the room.

I was in mid-bow when I realized the accolades weren't for me.

Chelsea had taken cheese to the next level.

Literally.

She had constructed a Charcuterie Chateau, which included a prosciutto-wrapped chimney, olive-lined roof, and Parmesan snowflakes descending from above.

Was Chelsea pumping Parmesan through her vents?

Son of a bi***!

"Yours is nice too." Chelsea smiled at my one-dimensional display.

There is no shaming like cheese shaming.

But…

If she can make a cabin, I will build a village.

I had no choice but to borrow on our (non-cheese) house to pay for a multi-cheese complex.

Was I supposed to just let Chelsea out-cheese me yet again?

Exactly!

That year, I strutted into the party with a masterpiece.

"Ta-dah!" I announced, unveiling my Village de Fromage.

Eyes rolled.

Does no one say ta-dah anymore?

The women were too busy chanting, "Ten…nine…eight…" as a Charcuterie New Year's Eve ball dropped from the ceiling.

"Ta-dah!" Chelsea called.

Everyone applauded her aeronautical ball of cheese.

I stood deflated, like overcooked Brie.

But if you think I gave up, you're crazy.

Chelsea, that evil cheese genius, only made me stronger, and this past year, I did it!

My kids weren't happy about it, but when they stood in the middle of that party, covered head to toe in an assortment of the finest meats and cheeses, attached by toothpicks, the crowd went wild.

Quincey whined about being "lactose intolerant," but that pimento in her mouth shushed her right up.

Same with Parker when she complained about the toothpicks.

Had these kids never heard of acupuncture?

The guests gushed as they nibbled well-aged gouda off my children's limbs.

Chelsea cursed herself for not having kids and began slathering her Labradoodle in Gorgonzola.

I exchanged looks with the other women, and I know we were all thinking the same thing.

Too far, Chelsea, too far.

All the Single Ladies

Although I usually prefer comedy, sometimes I write about scary things like timeshare presentations or my kitchen cupboards or Sandy, the swim instructor.

Recently, I learned about a scenario so frightening, I had to write about it.

Dating.

You're probably thinking, *what does this lady know about dating?*

It's true, the last time I was a single lady, I had big hair and bitchin' leg warmers.

But even if I'm not in the singles scene, I know stuff.

Scary stuff.

For example, I recently heard about a friend's 22- year-old daughter who went on a date.

This Prince Charming suggested a boat ride.

A sunset cruise on a catamaran!

How romantic!

Except the catamaran was actually a paddle boat.

The kind where you must keep pumping your legs to make it go, so it feels less "datey" and more "forced labor-y."

But at least the harbor was beautiful.

Which is why halfway through the boat ride, the boy FaceTimed his mom.

Which meant he was too distracted to paddle, so the girl had to pump even harder until her legs cramped up.

"Look how beautiful the sunset is," the boy said.

"It sure is," his mom replied.

But that's not even the frightening part.

The girl went out with this MotherLover AGAIN!

This time he took her to a Paint Night.

It was at a local brewery, where canvases and paint brushes were set up for the guests.

The two of them took a seat, and MotherLover said, "I have a surprise for you!"

And that's when he introduced her to his mom.

The three of them spent several minutes chatting in a relaxed Greek tragedy type of way.

Then the girl excused herself to go to the bathroom.

When she returned Mom had taken her seat and MotherLover said, "You don't mind sitting over there, do you?"

The girl was relocated to a seat in the far corner of the room.

Meanwhile, Mom and MotherLover painted and giggled and "oohed" and "aahed" over each other's pictures.

Occasionally, the boy waved to the girl.

But the girl didn't notice because she was busy drawing a melancholy self-portrait, like many artists do.

The good news is she didn't cut off her ear.

But if you think that was the end, you're wrong!

There was a THIRD DATE!

It involved a nice dinner and wonderful conversation.

I heard it went well.

The girl wasn't invited.

Perfectly Respectable Chompers

When this quarantine started, I looked in the mirror and said, "Hey, YOU, this is your opportunity, YOU CAN DO IT!"

When trying to motivate oneself, it's important to speak in loud and encouraging tones.

Back in March, I made a list of goals.

Write a novel, run a marathon, make sourdough from a starter...

(Haven't started, too long, they sell bread at the store.)

But this was my greatest disappointment by far.

"Tomorrow, definitely tomorrow," was what I kept telling myself.

Then, yesterday, it happened.

The Grim Reaper called.

"How about Monday at ten?" She asked.

"Okay," I said, sniffling.

The 11th hour had arrived.

It was time to floss.

Yes, it's true.

My name is January, and I don't floss.

Except the night before a dental appointment.

Now, before you get all high and mighty and think I'm some swamp ogre, you should know…

I have perfectly respectable chompers.

They're straight, they're white, they're clean.

I just don't like to floss.

It feels abusive.

And after I floss for the first time in months, it looks abusive.

Like I went ten rounds with Rocky. And I didn't win.

(Of course, I didn't win. It's Rocky!)

"Maybe try mint-flavored floss," my friend Kim suggested.

Lisa, another pro-flosser, added, "I like Listerine."

"The mouthwash?" I asked.

They shook their heads.

The two of them threw out more recommendations: Glide, Tom's, Oral-B (hey, that's the one I use twice a year!), Radius Vegan Soft Floss…

They're making vegan dental floss?

Are we supposed to be eating our floss?

If so, I'd like mine bacon-flavored.

"I've had the same Oral-B forever," I told them.

Sigh.

"You know floss expires?" Lisa said.

This flossing seminar had given me a lot to think about.

Sunday night, I took out my elderly floss.

How did it go?

I guess as well as any crime scene goes.

Monday morning, I arrived at 9:45.

Best to impress with punctuality as I would soon be disappointing them.

Once I got settled in the chair, my dentist, Dr. B., began prodding my gums with a smaller version of what the Grim Reaper carries.

He then used his one non-threatening tool, the adorable doll mirror, to get a closer look.

After a few "hmms," he removed the instruments and smiled.

"So, have we been flossing?" He asked.

One of us has.

I nodded. "Yep, definitely. I mean, not all the time, but uh...sometimes...Can we turn down that light?"

"It's important to floss," he said, reaching for his ultrasonic cleaning drill.

(My flossing friends had never heard of this tool. Apparently, this is the punishment for us non-flossers.)

The drill revved to life with the sound of a Texas chainsaw.

But not as soothing.

For the next thirty minutes my teeth and I enjoyed Dr. B's favorite game, Sadistic Plaque Exploration.

PLEASE STOP! I'LL FLOSS! I PROMISE!

Finally, we moved on to polishing.

Awe, the sweet relief of minty gravel.

"You can rinse," Dr. B said, signifying we were done.

I picked up the Dixie Cup of Listerine. "Did you know Listerine makes floss?"

He smiled.

I was fooling no one.

And then it occurred to me.

The dentist/patient relationship has to be the most dysfunctional of all relationships.

I lie to you. You torture me. I give you money.

Six months later, you send me a postcard with Dancing Molars, and we do it all over again.

Leaving the office, I peered inside my plastic bag of goodies.

A green toothbrush.

My favorite color!

Colgate Toothpaste.

Travel size, fun!

A pamphlet on Gum Health.

I know what I'll be reading tonight!

And...

Oral-B Floss.

See you in six months.

Chapter 11 - It Only Took Me Half a Century

Some things they don't teach you in school. Or maybe, they do. I wasn't paying attention.

Eyebrows

It was about a year and a half ago, and both Quincey and Parker were home for Christmas. As we were getting ready to go out for dinner, I noticed Parker was doing something to her eyebrows.

Was she coloring them? Was that a marker? Why would she do this?

"This is an eyebrow pencil," she explained. "Some of us like to have eyebrows."

"I have eyebrows," I said.

Both my daughters shook their heads. I looked in the mirror and pointed to the blonde fuzz that rested above my eyes. "What do you call these?"

"Sad," my oldest daughter, Quincey said.

I studied my barely visible middle-aged eyebrows. I looked at my daughters' perfect brown arches.

Good God, they were right! Why hadn't I noticed this atrocity? Why hadn't anybody ever said anything? Or were they saying stuff behind my back? I bet my nickname was No Eyebrows.

"Okay," I whispered to Parker. "Can you give me eyebrows?"

"You don't need to whisper," she said, taking the cap off her eyebrow pen. "We're not doing anything illegal."

Well, maybe not illegal, but bordering on scandalous. This was all very exciting.

She pushed my bangs back and positioned the pen on the top of my pseudo-eyebrow. Slowly, she traced one brow, then the other. She took a step back, nodded, and smiled.

"So much better," Parker said.

"Congratulations, Mom," Quincey added. "You now have eyebrows."

I walked over to the mirror.

"AAAAH!"

I resembled Uncle Leo from *Seinfeld*, when Elaine drew his eyebrows with magic marker after he singed them off.

Uncle Leo was not the look I was going for.

"They're so dark," I said, staring at this bold addition on my face.

"Trust me," Parker said. "You just need to get used to them."

And she was right.

For the next few hours, I kept checking out my new eyebrows and by the end of the night, my initial horror had been replaced with adoration.

It was like my eyes had been waiting their whole lives for that special something to complete them, a special something called eyebrows.

Worse Than Labor

Recently, I survived an ordeal so filled with physical anguish and emotional trauma, I swore I'd never do it again. Having a baby? Worse: a triathlon. At least during labor, an epidural is an option.

When I signed up for my first triathlon, I thought, "How hard could it be?" I can swim. I can bike. I can run.

And besides, it was only a Sprint or "baby" triathlon --750-meter swim, 20-kilometer bike, 5-kilometer run— as opposed to an Olympic or Ironman distances, which range from "long" to "are you insane?"

Parker, who's a member of the Cal Poly SLO triathlon team, convinced me to sign up for the Lake Lopez triathlon in March. It was early January and I had ten weeks to train. No problem.

For the first month, my training consisted of telling others about my upcoming race. Then, with only six weeks to go, I got serious.

I bought a new running shirt.

With four weeks left, I finally started working out. Unfortunately, I trained as if my event was a three-day festival, with snacks and siestas in between. I'd swim on Fridays, bike on Saturdays, and run on Sundays. Never once did it occur to me, "Hey imbecile, when you're done swimming, see how it feels to immediately get on that bike, and when you finish that, try some running."

As race day neared, I was filled with a mixture of anticipation, high hopes, and delusion. Reality set in the morning of the race.

At the registration tent, I was greeted by a perky young girl. "Are you a volunteer?" she asked.

That was the first sign that this triathlon might not go well.

There were others.

The lake was so cold my face refused to make contact with the water, and I ended up dog paddling 750 meters. (Perhaps I should have trained in something other than a heated pool.)

Halfway through the swim, a fellow swimmer had to loosen my wetsuit because I was feeling claustrophobic and on the verge of a panic attack. (Upside: new friend.)

On more than one occasion, the lifeguard on the paddle board asked, "Are you sure you're okay?"

When I finally dragged myself onto shore, the emcee announced, "Well, it looks like the last of the swimmers are finally coming in."

After the swim, instead of wrapping myself in a towel and curling into the fetal position (why can't *that* be the second leg of a triathlon?), I now had to ride for twenty kilometers…on a mountain bike, which I had convinced myself was just as good as a road bike.

It wasn't.

Which was probably why that 75-year-old woman I saw earlier and thought, "Dear Lord, I hope she can do this," passed me by.

Not to mention the bikers in front of me kept getting smaller and smaller.

Eventually, the only ones left on the course were the volunteers. One just yelled, "You can do it." It was more a question than a statement.

When I finally pedaled into the transition area, teary-eyed and sweaty, a photographer took my picture. Thank you for capturing my misery.

But the misery wasn't over.

It was time to run a 5K, and with the strength of a newborn deer, I was off.

The course was uphill on the way out. The course was uphill on the way back. Towards the end, it was just me and the guy in the truck, picking up the cones. (Upside: He did not pass me.)

There, miraculously, in the not-too-far-off-distance, was the finish line. As I crossed it, the 75-year-old woman cheered for me.

Thirty minutes later, my bruised ego and I departed.

"Thanks for volunteering!" someone yelled.

"Never again," I said.

Then, last week I got an email for another triathlon. The swim promised semi-warm conditions.

Yeah, right.

The bike course was hailed as scenic.

Not a chance.

The run was guaranteed to be flat.

Well…maybe.

Fractured Tales: The MRI

I had an MRI last week.

After checking in, Jason, the technician, led me to the back waiting room.

I took a seat.

"Hmmm," Jason said, looking over my chart. "It says here that you are signed up for the Tesla 1.5 MRI…*not* the Tesla 3 MRI."

"What's the difference?" I asked.

"The Tesla 3 has a stronger signal and better resolution." He scratched his head. "Your doctor *always* prefers the Tesla 3."

How dare my doctor prescribe me the vastly inferior Tesla 1.5!

Was I not worthy of the Tesla 3?

"Do you want me to see if I can get you on the Tesla 3?" Jason asked.

That's like asking an airline passenger, *"Would you like to move to first class?"*

Uh, duh

"Yes, please," I said.

I breathed a sigh of relief.

Can you believe I almost settled for the Tesla 1.5?

Thank God for Jason!

Jason returned a minute later. "Sorry, the Tesla 3 is not available."

Jason then escorted me to the low budget MRI room.

He had me lay down on an econo table.

The subpar Tesla 1.5 sluggishly slid into place.

Jason handed me a rubber ball that resembled a turkey baster, attached to a cord. "This is your panic button."

I bet the Tesla 3 has a "We're having fun" button.

"We'll get started in a minute," he said.

"I'm kind of hungry," I told Jason, as he was leaving the room.

Nothing.

Not even a bag of peanuts.

A minute later, the machine roared to life.

It began with the whooshing noise of an ultrasound, accompanied by the pulsating beat of an EDM concert and finished off with the sweet melody of jackhammering for the deaf.

Whoever composed the musical score for the Tesla 1.5 made some odd choices.

I closed my eyes, hoping it would end soon.

When it was over, Jason walked me back to the waiting room and let me know that my blurry, low-resolution, sub-standard MRI results would be ready in three to four days.

I slumped out of the building.

If only I'd never heard of the Tesla 3 MRI.

Thanks a lot, Jason.

From the Gecko

There is no such expression as *"from the gecko."* I have used this wrongly worded phrase my entire adult life. I'd make such remarks as, "That was doomed to fail, *from the gecko.*" Or "They seemed perfect for each other, *from the gecko.*" For over thirty years, I made these comments out loud, to multiple people. Why didn't anybody ever correct me? Or did everybody else also think a lizard was involved?

It wasn't until about a year ago, a friend finally said, "You know, it's not *from the gecko;* it's *from the get-go."*

"From the get-go," I nodded, digesting this new information. "Like it happened from the very beginning."

Yeah, that made more sense.

My Above Average Colon

Last week I did something I've never done before.

Bungee jump? Swim with sharks? Take shots off a stranger's body?

Not exactly.

Though, there was drinking involved.

A bottle of magnesium citrate, followed by sixty-four ounces of MiraLAX consumed in twenty-minute intervals.

We'll call it Happy Hour.

The fun didn't stop there. This was followed by a trip to my local surgery center where doctors inserted instruments (surgical, not musical) into certain orifices…you get the idea.

I had my first colonoscopy.

(Aren't you glad this isn't a picture book?)

I had been dreading this procedure for months and was becoming increasingly anxious. When I get anxious, I over-share. The week of the procedure, it was all I could talk about.

"I'm having my first colonoscopy," I said.

"That's nice," the Amazon guy responded. "If you could just sign here."

"I've heard the day before is the worst," I told a woman at Target.

"Oh, really…" she trailed off, switching lines.

"Thank God for anesthesia," I said.

"Si," my gardener nodded, and returned to mowing the lawn.

The real fun started two days before the procedure. I was instructed to drink a bottle of magnesium citrate at 6 p.m. It was almost 6 and I hadn't had dinner.

Like Jesus and death row inmates, I was about to embark on my last supper.

The nurse, whom I had spoken to earlier, recommended a light dinner.

Did she forget I wouldn't be eating for almost two days? Did I mention I was starving? Did she even know what she was talking about?

Fettuccini Alfredo it is.

After dinner, I sat down and opened a 2019 bottle of magnesium citrate.

I sniffed. "Mm, citrus."

I took a sip. "Mm, tar."

It took me over an hour to gulp down the entire bottle. Within minutes, the tarry substance coated my insides; I was bloated and nauseous. It took several hours before the magnesium and fettuccini stopped waging war in my stomach.

I guess the nurse *did* know what she's talking about.

The next day was a blur of broth and green Jell-O.

More than anything, I dreaded the evening. I would, once again, be forced to consume mass quantities of nauseating liquids.

That night, teary-eyed and trembling, I mixed MiraLAX into sixty-four ounces of Gatorade and took a swig.

Holy crap, it was delicious!

MiraLAX is an odorless powder, so it was basically detox Gatorade. Throw in a few orange slices and we might as well be at a soccer game.

The next morning, I checked into the Surgical Center. After filling out paperwork, the receptionist said, "Now, you do have the option of local anesthesia, where you would be semi-conscious and feel some things."

Who are the people choosing this option?

Perhaps these are the people thinking, *hmm, you know who I've always wanted to meet...My colon.*

I don't have that desire. I trust that my colon is in the correct location, doing the things a colon should be doing. And if that's not the case, the doctor can tell me about it later.

"I'd like to be unconscious and feel nothing," I told the receptionist.

She nodded and added, "There is an additional charge for general anesthesia."

"What's that?" Steve piped up.

"You can't put a price on comfort," I said.

The bill we received later said otherwise, but still, worth every penny.

Once in pre-op, I was given a gown (not formal) and some warm fuzzy socks.

"Mm, cozy," I told the nurse, wiggling my toes in the socks. "Do I get to keep these?"

She gave me a look.

Am I the only one who thinks soft socks would make for the perfect colonoscopy party favor?

The nurse wheeled me into the surgical room. "The doctor will be in shortly."

"And the anesthesiologist?" I asked.

"She'll be here in a minute."

I breathed a sigh of relief. I know most people think the doctor is the star, but to me, the anesthesiologist is the true headliner.

A few minutes later, the anesthesiologist entered the room. "I'm Dr. Abdul."

"I love you," I whispered.

Moments later, an IV was inserted and something wonderful called Propofol trickled into my bloodstream. A nurse counted, "Ten, nine, eight …"

Like Snow White, I took a good nap.

Unlike Snow White, there were no dwarfs, princes, or magical kisses.

Who knows, maybe there were?

That stuff was great. In fact, when I came to, I was tempted to ask for more.

Are you sure we're done? Do you want to check out some other organs? Come back, Dr. Abdul!

A few days later, the doctor called with the results.

"No polyps and your colon is in good shape."

I wasn't surprised. I've always felt I had an above average colon.

Unfortunately, I didn't fully recover. My post procedure headaches and nausea had diminished, but everything I ate was going right through me.

When I told my doctor, she responded, "Well, that's not good."

That's not a phrase you want to hear from your doctor.

After a few days, we got some answers.

"You have E. coli," my doctor confirmed.

Well, that's a crummy party favor.

She explained I had most likely contracted it from the instruments used at the surgical center. Next time I'll remember to ask for the *sterile* instruments.

My daughter panicked when I told her. "Oh my God, you're going to die!"

"E. coli," I enunciated. "Not EBOLA."

Turns out E. coli can be bad, but in non-medical terms, I contracted the not-so-bad kind.

Within a few days, my symptoms subsided, and I was finally on the road to recovery. The best news was that my above average colon and I wouldn't have to make an appearance for another ten years.

Hallelujah!

No more pesky doctors inserting instruments where they don't belong.

Then, last week, I received an appointment reminder card from my gynecologist.

And the fun continues…

Not MiraLAX

Acknowledgments:

To my husband, Steve, you are my rock, and I couldn't have done it without you. Thank you for believing in me and supporting me through this process. I so appreciate you being a calming voice when I needed it. I love you more than you know, and I swear, I'm thinking about dinner right now.

To my entire family, Steve, Parker, Quincey, Colby, Mom, Dad, Holland, and Noah, thank you for not only being my biggest fans, but also for allowing me to continuously write about you all, which I may or may not have occasionally embellished. I love you all!

To my blog editors, Quincey, Luann, and Mary, I cannot thank you enough for the countless hours you have put into reading and editing my stories. I also appreciate you putting up with my overused asterisks and my misplaced commas. (Yes, I lack comma sense.) I couldn't have done it without you.

To my dear friends, Catherine, Chris, Chriss, Denise, Donna, Jacki, Jen, Jill, Juliana, Julie, Kim, Linda, Lisa B., Lisa J., Lisa S. (so many Lisas!), Lorraine, Melita, and Michele, thank you for consistently reading, sharing, and even inspiring my stories. I am so grateful for your support and enthusiasm, but mostly I am grateful for your friendship.

To my publisher, Donna, you are a joy to work with and your professionalism, feedback, and encouragement has made this journey such a positive experience. Most importantly, thank you for believing in this book and helping bring it to life

To my wonderful editor, Kathy, you taught me to let go of asterisks (well, most of them) and educated me on ellipses. What more could a girl ask for? Thank you for your hard work and encouragement.

To all my Midlifebloomer followers, who have read, shared, and commented on my stories, your words of encouragement mean more than you know.

About the Author:

January Ornellas started writing short, humorous stories about her midlife adventures in 2018. In 2019, she launched her blog, Midlifebloomer, which she continues to write for today. Since then, she has had many of these stories published (LA Times, Chicken Soup for the Soul, Erma Bombeck Writers' Workshop) and was an honorable mention in the 2022 EBWW global humor writing competition. Ornellas is currently working on a new book, *Diabolical*, a dark comedy about softball moms who terrorize the 10 and Under girls' softball diamond. When she is not writing, Ornellas enjoys running, gardening, traveling, and spending time with family and friends. She lives in Moorpark, CA with Steve, her husband of 33 years.